RIDING D

The process of learning and i   ⌐

Kerry Turner

First published in Great Britain in 2007 by

Kerry Turner

ISBN 978-0-9557084-0-4

Illustrations by Anne Fenn

Causal Loop Diagrams by Kerry Turner

Design by Kerry Turner

Printed and bound in France by Nouvelles Presses du Centre, Limoges

Table of Contents

Foreword 7
1 Introduction 9
    What is this book about? 9
    Who can benefit? 10
    Why did I want to write this book? 11
    Introducing the author 12
    The Survey 13
    How the book is structured 15
    Acknowledgements 17
2 The Objectives of Riding 18
    Control or influence? 19
    Achieving self control 23
    Systems and riding 24
    Communication 26
3 Understanding Dynamics 29
    Structure affects behaviour 29
    Mental Models 31
    Variables and Relationships 32
    Digging deeper 34
    Feedback 36
    Equilibrium 42
    Improvement 43
4 Connection in Theory 47
    Rider Ingredients 49
    Strengthening the connection 52
    Influencing the horse's ingredients 54
5 Connection in Practice 58
    Hands 58
    An Independent Seat 77
    Legs 83
6 Communication 89
    Balance 89
    Communication - Correction and Reward 96
    Definiteness 104
7 The Dynamics of Training 107
    Correct musculature 107

The Scales of Training 112
The Way Forward 123
8 Rider Dynamics 125
Brain control 126
Inside vs Outside 128
Body control 129
Back problems 131
Pilates 132
Alexander Technique 134
Nutrition for riding 138
Fitness for riding 138
9 Application - Riding in the moment 140
Dismounted preparation 140
Thoughts on lunging 141
Initial Assessment and warm up 144
Down to work 146
Training opposites 150
Cool-down 151
Some thoughts on riding exercises 152
Circles 153
Going sideways 154
Improving the Canter 156
Improving the Trot 158
Developing the Whole 161
Training and competition 162
10 Managing your performance 164
Finding the right horse 165
Choosing a trainer 171
Assessment and Feedback 178
Prioritisation 182
11 Thoughts on Equipment 186
Horse equipment 186
Bits 186
Nosebands 189
Saddles 191
Numnahs and girths 194
Lunge Tack and facilities 200

Shoes 201
Rider equipment.. 202
Riding surfaces... 203
12 The Way Forward – The Learning Rider 206
The Learning Cycle 208
Improving Learning effectiveness................................211
Knowledge acquisition 213
Active reading 214
Filtering knowledge 215
The Learning Zone 216
Adaptation... 221
Afterword... 226
Appendix 1 - References... 228
Appendix 2 - Survey questions..................................... 231
Appendix 3 – Pilates.. 233
Appendix 4 - Osteopathy.. 239
Appendix 5 - Massage.. 246
Biographies 248

For Shantie, without whom this project would not have been started.

Foreword

In this book Kerry Turner has challenged the rider - not just to improve but to really **"think"** about what they are doing.

It is clear throughout that the author believes that the good rider should be a lifelong student of this absorbing art and it is because I wholeheartedly agree with her that I am delighted to write this Foreword.

Riding is an art that involves another living being, the horse, who is as unique and individual as us. The difference between the rider and the horse is that the horse is not a volunteer. As a result we owe it to him to constantly strive to improve our skills and "connection" with him if his welfare is to be uppermost in our hearts and minds, which should be the case for all good horsemen.

All too often good horsemanship is sadly measured by how many competitions have been won or difficult horses conquered, when in reality it should be measured by a state of peaceful agreement and co-operation between horse and rider - in other words HARMONY.

Good harmony can only be achieved by understanding oneself first and then the horse, along with a sound grasp of technical skills. When the rider is truly aware of this and is committed to constantly strive to improve, only then can he or she reap the rewards this lifelong journey will bring.

I know that by reading this book your own and your individual horse's journey can only be enhanced.

Patrick Print FBHS
Chairman
The British Horse Society
July 2007

A big thank you to **Dodson & Horrell Limited,** who partially funded the costs of printing this book.

Dodson & Horrell Limited was founded in Ringstead, Northamptonshire, in 1939 and is still a family run business to this day, Dodson & Horrell has grown to become Europe's leading horse feed manufacturer. In addition to the highly successful horse feed range, Dodson & Horrell also manufactures the Chudleys range of dog and pet food.

The company is committed to all aspects of animal nutrition and was proud to see its Royal Warrant status extended to that of horse and dog feed manufacturers to HM Queen Elizabeth II in September 2006.

1 Introduction

What is this book about?

This book is about understanding the dynamics of riding. Literally, what is happening when we ride. If we can understand the dynamics of riding we can make better riding choices, and improve the effectiveness of our riding. I believe that riding is an activity of the whole self – the mind and the body. So to improve our riding we have to develop our whole self, both our mind and our body.

Ultimately we are what we think. We can have the best body and riding skills but unless we believe this we have nothing. Riding develops and tests our self control. Each moment we ride brings a new test. To ride really well we must learn to rise above all tests. We have to "know" riding in our mind and really trust ourselves to achieve our full riding potential.

To "know" we have to learn. We never stop learning. It is a lifetime's task. We are constantly refining and improving our knowledge. This book aims to develop the concept of a "Learning Rider" and to help the reader to become one. A Learning Rider is a rider who is driven to perpetually deepen her understanding of the horse/rider interaction and to use that understanding for the benefit of all riders and horses.

We are all individuals, and unique. Our horses are all individuals, and unique. This means that we have to understand *our self* and *our horse*. What works for me may not work for you. We have to seek out and find what works for us and create our own recipe for riding success. This news is either exciting and liberating, or daunting, depending which way you look at it. But it is the truth.

Nowadays we see riders focussing too much on what I call the "outside" of themselves (their position/appearance) and of their horse (outline). Corrections which only influence the outside will never succeed in the longer term. They will not last. Sustainable improvement comes from the inside. When the rider develops the inside of themselves; their mind (understanding) and their body (balance, strength, flexibility), and the inside of their horse, the improvements are lasting. Then and only then will the outside be as it should be and sustainably so.

Fortunately there are tools and techniques to help us in our quest. Read on to discover more.

Who can benefit?
Stand outside any swimming pool and ask the people coming out with wet hair what they have been doing. Invariably they will look at you a little funny and say "swimming". But this single word masks a whole spectrum of skills and motivations. For some their swimming is a social activity; for others it is for physical well-being (health and fitness); for others it is because they have been told that they should swim.

Watch the swimmers in the pool. Many of these swimmers aren't really swimming; they are simply managing to stay afloat between two points. They are content with this definition of swimming or perhaps they believe that's all there is. Either way they have no interest in improving their swimming; in really knowing swimming.

It is the same in the riding arena. If you are happy with the effectiveness of your riding then this book is not for you. This book is for people who are seeking to progress their riding and realise their potential. Perhaps you are struggling to find the right way forward...or a top competitor looking for new ideas and inspiration.

It follows that this book is not about "learning how to stay on a horse" and therefore it is not for absolute beginners. I subscribe to the school that says that absolute beginners are better to throw away the books and let the horse teach them to feel what it is like to ride.

All riders (including beginners) are horse trainers. This is because when we are with a horse we are training him whether we like it or not. Good riders know this, bad riders either don't think or don't care.

Good riders also know that training is a two-way process. The horse trains us just as much as we train him. He trains us in the art of self control. He can bring out the best or the worst in us. *Choose to let him bring out the best and what you will learn will benefit you in all walks of life.*

Why did I want to write this book?
I write when I become so excited about something that it has to find an "outlet" or I would burst. Writing is my release. It also helps me to clarify and confirm my thinking as I have to structure my thoughts so that I can explain them to others.

I also wanted to give something back. To whom? To horses and their people. I feel that by sharing this thinking with people like you I can benefit people and horses in the developed world. Equally, by using the book to raise funds for an international horse charity, The Brooke Organisation, I am benefiting equines in less developed countries and therefore the people who depend on them for their livelihood. And by buying this book you are too.

I chose to publish this book myself for two reasons. Firstly, because it enables me to generate more profit for charity (as opposed to the shareholders in a publishing company). And secondly, because I wanted to maintain the integrity of my words. I know many authors whose words have lost their original meaning through the editing process.

This book will undoubtedly be improved on in future; perhaps by me, perhaps by someone else. I know this because I have struggled to draw a line under what I include in the book now. Every day brings new discoveries I am anxious to share. So this is a record of my thinking based on what I have learnt up to now. It is all any book ever can be.

Along the way I have made choices about the look and feel of the book as this affects the production costs and consequently the price of the book and the money I raise for charity. Perhaps I have made some compromises on look and feel that may make the book less attractive to read. I ask you to bear with this and forgive me for it. Being an unknown author has a price.

Introducing the author
I learnt to ride when I was 11 years old. I spent my 50p a week pocket money on hiring a pony from a local farmer for an hour every Saturday morning. I rode over there on my trusty bike, equipped with a riding hat my dad had found in a ditch, a new crop and the Ladybird "Learn to Ride" book (which I still have today). I handed over the cash, tacked up the pony and went out into the field. Every so often I would stop and get the book out of my pocket to work out what to do next.

Eventually the farmer retired and I went on to helping out at a local stables in return for rides. I ate, slept and dreamt "pony" and eventually, at 14 years old, my parents saw that this was no passing phase and bought me a pony of my own.

We had no experience. I wanted the first pony I saw as I was terrified that they would change their minds. "Copper" was the result – a 13.2hh Chestnut cob-type pony, nappy and lacking in "jump". He was my pal for 2 years. I outgrew him and sold him to another young girl.

I then concentrated on school and exams...through 'O' levels, 'A' levels and University...gaining a First class Degree in Maths and a Masters in Operational Research (maths for business). I started work as a management consultant and worked hard to build my career...through this period equines were far from my mind.

At the age of 28, Graham, my long suffering partner, said "you're boring, you need a hobby, why don't you start riding again?" He bought me a hat and some riding lessons at a local riding school for my birthday. The inevitable happened. The old yearnings were rejuvenated. After a year I bought my first horse – a 7 year old Palomino part-bred Arab gelding with a hell of a jump called "Shantie". I still have him today. He is enjoying his retirement.

I changed to part-time work in order to concentrate on my riding and competed at the weekends (mainly show-jumping). I took a career break and went to study BHS Stages at Moulton College. I studied to Stage 4 but failed my Stage 3 Riding. I started eventing and discovered I let myself down on the dressage.

I guess that's where I started my quest to improve. I tried a succession of trainers, 2 new horses (one too small, the other too nasty), and BD Judge Training. I had glimpses of "great feelings" that were tantalising – but I never knew where they had come from or how to recreate them. I accepted these feelings as random. So random they stayed.

My strength is in analysing, learning and communicating – taking information from lots of sources; processing it; testing it; understanding connections; drawing conclusions and presenting them in ways which make things clearer. Ironically, I used this strength in my work but not in my riding or my home life.

In 2003 life became too much for me. I had a nervous breakdown. I left my career of twenty years and moved to France with Graham to start a long journey of self-discovery. For the first time I began to exercise the analytical skills I applied at work in my riding and my life. I started to really learn. About myself.

The riding process stopped being random. I started to understand what worked and why it worked. What didn't work and why it didn't work. I started to "know" riding. I wanted to share it with everyone. Partly so it could be discussed and partly to reinforce my own learning – to know that I know. I hope that you can see this and that this book can help you to make discoveries that work for you.

Shantie had an injury that meant I had to retire him from serious training, and I bought a lovely young horse, "Eric" a six year old pure-bred Lusitano gelding. We continue to learn and grow together here in this idyllic part of the world. This book marks the end of one chapter in my life and the beginning of a new one.

The Survey
In addition to learning by applying my own methods, a lot of my experience has been gleaned from others. I have been particularly

influenced by the trainers I have worked with and by the books I have read. However, I am very conscious that this is a fraction of the knowledge that could be available to me.

To try to rectify this and to gain a broader, more balanced spectrum of views on riding and training, I created a questionnaire and sent it to a cross-section of well-known trainers, judges and riders. I also contacted various international federations and organisations in the hope that their members could assist me.

You can find the questions in the appendix. Why not take half an hour and write down your response to my questions? Don't think too hard. Write down what is in your mind...what you would say if asked the questions in an impromptu interview.

I contacted over 300 individuals and organisations. 28 were keen to help and went on to provide me with a completed written response or the opportunity to cover the questions in an interview. This relatively poor overall response rate masks some huge variations across the sample. Almost 40% of trainers and 20% of British Dressage judges (Lists 1 and 2) did respond. I am incredibly grateful to these individuals, a number of who continue to help me with this project.

I had hoped that perhaps I would gain a statistically significant sample of responses that I could go on to analyse overall findings and implications. This has not been possible given the limited response. Instead I have used quotes from the survey to illustrate the range of opinions on different topics. Some day I hope that an equine organisation will properly fund and support a project like this to enable us all to benefit.

How to use this book
First of all you must read it. This is no coffee table book. And you must experiment and try out the ideas I am presenting. See if they work for you. Ask yourself - am I convinced this is worth a try? If it is then try it out.

Have no expectations. See what happens. Think about why it happened. Have another go.

Tell your horse about it. He'll help you out.

Buy yourself an exercise book or a large diary with a page per day. At the end of each day, or the morning after, write down what you think happened and what you learnt. In this way you will write your own book of riding.

I want this book to really make you think. There are questions for you to answer all the way through. You will only receive the full benefit if you use them.

I want to encourage you to never regard any word as sacrosanct, whether written or spoken. Seek the truth, ask questions, challenge, experiment… take responsibility for your own learning…and start to do it now. The world will never be the same again. Trust me and try it. Read on and become a Learning Rider…

How the book is structured
Chapter 1 introduces the book and the author.

Chapter 2 encourages the reader to examine why they ride. Only by being clear about why we are doing things can we make better choices and act in ways consistent with achievement.

Riding well is a complex process. To achieve our riding objectives we need to understand what helps us to make progress, what gets in the way *and* all the cause and effect relationships between them. To help with this, in Chapter 3 we consider a simple thinking tool called Systems Thinking. It is a powerful way of understanding the dynamics of riding.

Our ability to influence our horse is impacted by the strength of our connection with him. Chapter 4 analyses these connections and suggests how they may be improved.

Chapter 5 looks at the physical implications of connecting with your horse. Specifically, it considers all the aspects of contact.

Strong connections provide us with the possibility of improved communication. But what do we communicate about and how? These are the topics for Chapter 6.

The previous 3 chapters have considered the rider's influence on a trained horse. How do we go about improving a horse? Chapter 7 considers alternative training approaches and analyses some of the pre-eminent texts on training.

Chapter 8 considers how the rider can improve her riding effectiveness. Riding involves our whole self. To do it well we need to use our body and our mind. So we have to learn about ourselves, about our body and mind, to use them more effectively and efficiently.

Chapter 9 looks at what actually happens when we mount our horse with the aim of training him. It brings together the concepts presented in previous chapters and demonstrates the practical application on horseback – literally, riding in the moment.

Chapter 10 encourages the rider to take responsibility for her own performance improvement and provides some techniques that can help as well as discussing finding the most suitable equine and trainer partners.

Chapter 11 examines the controversial topic of equipment for horse and rider training and provides some opinions.

Chapter 12 considers how the reader can continue to progress by adopting the habits of the continuously improving "Learning Rider".

Acknowledgements
Of the many people who have influenced me over the years I would like to especially mention:
My Trainers: Inger Bryant, John Micklem, Gloria Pullen, Jean Halls, Trudi Dempsey, Sophie Volet
My Family: Gerald and Beryl Turner and Graham Hey
My Horses: Shantie, Eric, and all those I have ridden over the years
My horsey pals: Anita Thomas, Paula Shirreff, Pauline Smith, Chris Shelton and Judy Pickerill
Dennis Sherwood, Sarah Bell and my many colleagues over the years at Deloitte Haskins & Sells, Coopers & Lybrand, PriceWaterhouseCoopers and IBM. And, of course, my consulting clients who provided so much food for thought.

For help with this book I must thank:
Anne Fenn for creating the illustrations in figures 1,2,6,12,13,16,17,19, 20, 21,22,27,30,31,32,34,36,38.
Graham Hey for proof reading and help with layout.

Special thanks must also go to all those who gave their time and knowledge by responding to my survey and completing the questionnaire.

Finally, thank you to those who took the time to share their thinking in the texts I have used to help me with this book. I now know how hard this task can be. References to the texts I have used are marked by (#) and a complete reference is given in Appendix 1.

2 The Objectives of Riding

> "We want to understand the nature of the horse, respect his personality and not suppress it throughout his training. Then we are on the right way" Dr Reiner Klimke to his daughter Ingrid (13)

In Chapter 1 I explained that this book is for those who want to improve their riding. If I had used the term dressage in chapter 1 instead of riding I expect that many of you would switch off. "Dressage is only for experienced riders". "It's for competition". "It's not for me". But whether we like it or not all riders are involved in dressage.

How so? Dressage is a French word with a simple meaning. It means training. As we learnt in chapter 1 all riders are horse trainers. Whenever we spend time with or on a horse we are influencing him and therefore training him.

What is the objective of dressage – of training the horse? I think that this is a very important question for us all to ask ourselves. Take a moment and think what this means for you. Why do you seek to improve yourself and your horse?

The Federation Equestre Internationale (FEI) states "The object of dressage is the development of the horse into a happy athlete through harmonious education. As a result, it makes the horse calm, supple, loose and flexible, but also confident, attentive and keen, thus achieving perfect understanding with his rider."(1)

Patrick Print (FBHS, Chairman BHS) expressed his thoughts for me very succinctly. "For enjoyment. To have a happy horse and rider".

Inger Bryant (List 1 Dressage Judge) went further in explaining how this could be achieved. "First I aim to have the horse understand what we want and second to develop his physical ability."

A top competition rider's response was quoted in an article published on the internet. "First of all we seek to control the horse".

> *Do you agree? Do you seek to control your horse?*

Control or influence?

For me this question goes to the heart of a fundamental difference in philosophy amongst riders:

Do you seek to control or to influence, to dominate or to understand, to instruct or to communicate?

Do you see the aids as a means of communicating and connecting or as a means of control?

Do you see riding as an ability to stay on a horse and have the horse do what you want, or do you want to feel that the horse wants to do these things for you of his own free will?

Do you see your horse as your partner or as your servant?

Do you want him simply to do as he is told or do you want him to be involved in choices and able to express himself?

Do you look forward to schooling sessions as an interesting conversation with a good friend (win/win – you both come out feeling good) or do you seek obedience at any price (win/lose – only one of you feels good)?

Do you see yourself as your horse's teacher, his trainer, his best friend, his dancing partner, his sugar mummy?

Do you want what's best for him now or best for his long-term future?

One trainer I worked with (very briefly) explained his belief that it was important to see the horse as an enemy. Why? The more you hate him the better you will be able to do "the necessary". What is "the necessary" I hear you ask? Example one: Lean backwards on draw reins. Example two: lunge in tight side reins with random attempts to pull the horse over. Why? To disrupt his balance so he will look to the reins for support! At this point I very nearly gave up riding.

My work as a management consultant leads me to believe that the core components of effectiveness in people are –
Understanding (knowing what to do)
Skills/abilities (knowing how to do it) and
Motivation (knowing why to do it).

I believe that the most important of these is motivation. There can be high levels of "talent" (skills/abilities) but without the desire to use this we have nothing.

I think it is the same for all beings including horses. I think that what we riders are talking about when we use the terms control, obedience, acceptance and submission are in fact different levels of motivation. The highest level of motivation is passion. I want my horse to feel passionate about his work. Words like acceptance, obedience, tolerance and submission feel out of place in this context.

Why do I do dressage? For me the answer is for sheer joy and harmony. What do I mean by this? Exquisite moments of bliss where the whole has become more than the sum of the parts; where I feel as light as a feather; where the horse just senses what I want and responds effortlessly; a feeling of total connection to the horse, to myself, to life. It is a heavenly experience. At the base of this is a deep and meaningful relationship with my horse – one of mutual trust and respect – dare I say love? Together we become something more than either of us can be separately.

I've learnt from my survey that many others feel the same. I asked, how do you feel (in your mind and your body) when you are riding at your best? Here are some of the responses:

Euphoric! Like I am weightless and am floating.

Happy.

Joyful, and humble, I guess. My body feels powerful. The same way I guess a lot of people feel riding fast on a motorbike.

Effortless and supple.

Comfortable, calm, confident, controlled.

On top of the world!...everything flows as if by magic.

This is what happens when we have truly united with our horse. The whole has become more than the sum of the parts. It is effortless and sustainable. We have achieved total mind/body balance in movement. We have achieved so-called self-carriage, of mind and body.

How do you feel when you ride at your best? Have you felt the feeling I describe? Do you believe such a feeling is achievable for you?

To ride in this way we have to inhibit the human need to control and dominate and develop a trusting partnership of mutual understanding and forgiveness.

Why? In part because "control" is unachievable and therefore unrealistic. I know that I cannot control my horse. However, I do seek to influence him. I know that I can and do influence *every* thinking and feeling being that I come into contact with – whether I want to or not and whether I like it or not. And you do too!

Knowing this means that I have to take responsibility for the impact of my choices and actions...and this, in turn, means that I have to control myself. After all, the only living being I can truly control is myself. The secret of why I do dressage is that I discover and develop myself. I develop my mind and my body as they are the tools through which I can influence my relationship with my horse.

Which leads me to...the truth about control.
If you can't control yourself...you try to control your environment and those around you (including your horse). The more you are able to control yourself...the less you will feel the need to control your environment and those around you (including your horse).

"What do you mean control?" I hear you say. I am in control! But are you really? When confronted with a stimulus, do you think, consider all the options and choose before you respond. Or do you just respond?

By responding we give up our opportunity to choose. Responding is habitual and it shows a lack of self awareness and self control. There is always the opportunity to change this. But we have to really want to.

Influence requires contact. But that contact need not be physical. As a human being, I can influence another human being with words (spoken or written, face to face or mail/phone), with pictures (drawings, paintings, illustrations,photographs, films), with music, with verbal tones, with facial expressions, with body language, with touch, with actions, with behaviours.

We can sometimes develop a feeling of understanding with another human being such that we can read the other person because we know them so well. I can think of certain work colleagues where this has happened for me. We worked closely together for so long and understood each other perfectly. Communication becomes seemingly "telepathic". Others marvel at it and think it to be accidental. Those involved know there is no accident – only time and understanding ...good partnerships have to be worked at.

It is the same with a horse. We have to think about how we can influence him and develop our own personal communication system. A level of knowing that transcends the obvious.

Good communication is the foundation of a strong relationship. Stephen Covey, in his oft-quoted book "The Seven Habits of Highly Effective People" (2), states that good communication starts with listening. This means understanding the other person, before seeking to be understood yourself. I agree but would add that first we should seek to understand ourselves, then understand others, then seek to be understood.

Do you understand yourself?

I certainly didn't. I reached the age of 40 and probably knew more about business than about myself! At 41 I fell off the edge of the cliff in my mind. I wanted to physically fall off the edge of a cliff too but didn't have the guts.

I have thought a lot about what happened to me and how it happened, and have used the techniques I previously used to understand businesses on my own behaviour patterns and myself. It has been very revealing.

Only by understanding myself can I start to influence myself more positively to achieve self-control.

Achieving self control

Self control is not about suppressing (or depressing) feelings. It is not about becoming the stoical unflinching Englishman. Self control is about deciding how to respond and being consistent. It is about choice.

What do I mean when I say "myself"?

I have thought a lot about this question. I used to think that I was my brain. Now I realise that the body is important and if we don't look after it the brain is useless. I have also realised that I can control my brain – my thought patterns - and change them for the better. I can also control the amount of thought that is going on. I can calm my brain right down, not all the time but I am learning! This leaves me in a quandary. If *I* can control *my* body and *my* mind what am *I*?

Certainly I consist of lots of complicated cause and effect relationships working together to a common objective - to survive and thrive. I am more than the sum of my parts. I am a system.

If I were to break myself down into my constituent parts I would find lots of subsystems; systems of movement and control; a digestive and waste ejection system; a communication system; a reproductive system and so on. Each of these systems in isolation is not me. Only when these systems are connected and aligned to the common objective of keeping me alive do I exist.

It is the same when I become a subsystem of a larger system eg my family. This system will only become more than the sum of its parts when there is connection and alignment to common objectives. To improve a system we must seek to strengthen the connections and the alignment.

Systems and riding

The word "system" has many meanings. Some will think of a computer system. Some of bureaucracy. Others of a way of doing things, a methodology. In the context of this book the word system means "a set of interconnected and interacting entities that function as a whole to a common objective(s)." So a pile of fruit in a bowl is not a system. The tree which bore the fruit is. I am a system. My digestive system is a system. So is my horse. So is my family. So is the organisation I worked for. So is the World. So systems can be different sizes. We each have systems within us and belong to systems that are greater than us.

When we choose to ride our horse we aim to create a new system...when this system works perfectly it appears seamless and effortless. We have truly created a new system that is more than the sum of the parts. The feeling of harmony shows that the system is functioning well. The strength of the connections determines the strength of the system. We've all seen them – the partnerships who are truly in-sync, in harmony with each other. We've also seen the ones that aren't – a separate horse and a rider because the connections are not strong enough for harmony. To transcend the ordinary we have to understand and strengthen the connections.

"....the horse is an articulated system that must function as one unit. *Our final aim is to become united with that system.* Fluidity is just one element of this unity, made up of so many interrelated parts or elements that it requires deep study to comprehend it perfectly. "
Udo Burger (3)

The other test – what happens when you cut the system in half? If I cut myself in half I will die. Cut the horse and rider in half and you don't get two half-sized horse and riders! When horse and rider part company the system becomes two separate, and very different, systems - a horse and a human being. What was achievable when they were united is unachievable separated.

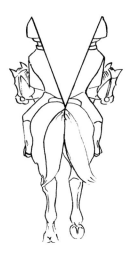

Figure 1 Half a system?

Systems are goal seeking. This means that they have a purpose. They seek balance or should I say equilibrium. If they get too much out of kilter they will push back. These are the laws of cause and effect. Whenever we work against the system rather than with it we may profit in the short term but we will always suffer in the longer term. Most quick fixes fail in the longer term. *ALL* our problems now are the results of choices made by our-selves and by others in the past. As Einstein observed, *"The significant problems we face cannot be solved at the same level of thinking we were at when we created them."*

Only by understanding the system can we make the right choices for the future. But we must recognise that our mission to understand the system will never end; the depth and width is incomprehensible. So we are all learners, we will never be 100% right, we can only make the best choice with our current level of understanding. And continuously seek to deepen and broaden that understanding. Every choice needs to be seen as an experiment to be monitored and learnt from. Did it work? What happened? Why? What should I do now? In this way we become perpetual learners and life becomes exciting.

Think for a moment. Why do people close their minds to learning?

Admitting the need to learn means admitting that we don't know. Not knowing is "uncool". We don't like to admit it. In addition, we associate learning with "effort". It is hard work.

At this point you may be saying "Not me. I know I'm useless..." Too much humility is not good either. It prevents us trying new things. It makes us indefinite. When things don't go to plan we blame ourselves rather than learning. I know. I've been there. We do need to be honest but maintain a positive attitude to our future learning.

Communication
The choices we make communicate our intentions and our values far more clearly than our words. Words can mislead. Behaviours are clear. My horses never lie and are never inconsistent because they have no words.

There is a saying "when in Rome...". A year ago I moved to rural France. To communicate with the people here I have to learn French. And I have to keep improving my French to improve my understanding and connection to French people. I can live here and be physically close to my French neighbours but I will never be truly connected in a deep mutual understanding until I speak French fluently.

It is the same for our horse. We choose to enter the horse's world. So we must communicate with our horse as a horse not as a human. When we choose to adopt a human attitude to the horse we will fail. We've all heard the words (or said them ourselves – I certainly have). "I work hard to keep him and I only ask for one hour of his attention each day...why won't he give me this". In the mental struggle we are not aware of the horse as a horse and that he lives truly in the moment and is truly honest. He doesn't do bargains and deals. He doesn't scheme and lie. He doesn't hold grudges. He doesn't love or hate. He is just a horse.

You may be able to fool assorted non-discerning others but you will never fool your horse or yourself. And what really matters at the end of the day? Not the rosettes or the ill-won accolades. What matters is how you really feel about yourself and your horse. You owe it to yourself, and your horse, to seek out the "real thing".

> *What are the qualities that define a good rider for you? Who do you admire and why?*

For me, the good rider gives her whole attention to her whole self. And she does the same for her horse. She helps him to become aware of his whole self. She creates situations where he can learn and feel. She encourages him to think for himself and to carry himself. She builds his confidence and his strength. She builds his trust in her.

There are so many parallels between riding and living. Riding provides the ultimate opportunity in learning to go with what is, to accept and relax into the movement. Not fighting it, not trying to make it into something else "the way I want it to be", just going with what is. Achieving transitions with as little disturbance to balance as possible.

We all want some stability as it is predictable and we know that we can cope. But too much and life would be boring; too little and life becomes like a helter-skelter ride. How much instability can we cope with? If we are fixed (rigid, inflexible) in our minds and bodies we are less able to ride life's waves. We have to learn to be more fluid, less rigid, more flexible.

Many people mistake this for "giving in" and associate this with "losing" or "failing", but I think it is better to see this as "accepting" and "releasing" ourselves from the chains of our own minds. FREE YOUR MIND. If we do cling on for too long eventually we do have to give in – or cave in – because our body can't cope with it and it collapses (breaks-down). "Accepting" isn't collapsing, it is releasing. In riding, as in life, we become strong by letting go, not by clinging on. Equally, we need to be strong to feel that we can let go.

Things to remember
The only thing I can truly control is myself.
Know yourself.
Don't react, make a conscious choice.
I am a system. My horse is a system.
When we choose to ride our horse we aim to create a new system.
The strength of the connections determines the strength of the system.
To make the right choices we must understand the system.
We become strong by letting go, not by clinging on.

3 Understanding Dynamics

Good riding is about uniting two very different systems; a human and a horse. When done well a new, beautifully harmonious system is formed. The whole is capable of more than the sum of the parts. This should be the aim of all riders: a harmonious equilibrium with their horse. To achieve this we must train our horse and ourselves to maintain this seamless system through movements that challenge the balance of the system.

Science has been applied to horse management in the fields of feeding, care and breeding but not, to my knowledge, to horse riding. Horse riding skill is often seen as a gift and, moreover, to be so much about feelings that science can't possibly play a part.

This book aims to dispel this myth and proposes an exposition of the cause and effect relationships at work. My belief is that if we understand the dynamics we can develop our horse and ourselves sustainably. And hopefully create the ultimate union of horse and human.

Structure affects behaviour
Take a look at the picture in Figure 2. What will happen when the girl pushes the domino closest to her?

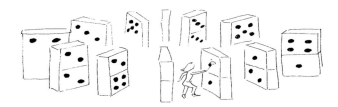

Figure 2 Dominoes

It's not a trick question! The dominoes will fall over in turn and unless the girl realises this and gets out of the way she is in for a nasty shock. Seeing the system (the dominoes and the way they inter-relate with each other) from where we're standing this is obvious. But maybe things look different from her stand-point? Maybe she sees the two dominoes close by but doesn't see the others or indeed how they could affect each other.

The key learning in this example is that the structure of a system (the component parts and how they inter-relate and affect each other) affects the behaviour of that system. This means that to influence the behaviour we must understand the structure of the system. What affects what, when and by how much. To do this we need to stand back and see the bigger picture. If we understand the structure we can think through what might happen when we pursue a course of action. In that way we can make better informed choices about which course of action to take. It follows that to make better decisions for the longer term, we need to be able to understand cause and effect relationships which are further apart in time and space.

The skill I am talking about here is thinking. This is what differentiates the human from other animals endowed with less good brains. Our horse and our dog understand cause and effect but only when closely connected. We exploit this when we train him "in the moment" by repetition. We can use our brain to think through and understand cause and effect over much greater expanses of space and time. It is this that we must exploit in ourselves as we seek to become better trainers.

If we see life as a stream of random events we are left feeling out of control and our only option is to react.

If we start to see patterns of events we can start to modify our behaviour and prepare. We are no longer caught unawares but we still don't feel in control.

When we understand the structure of cause and effect behind the patterns...then we know...and we can act confidently and in control.

Often we don't know with certainty what will happen when we change something. In fact I don't believe we can be 100% confident of anything! That doesn't mean we can't improve. We can make an educated guess and then establish experiments to understand further what happens if.........

Just as we use exercises to improve the strength of our bodies so we must use exercises to improve the strength of our brains. Systems Thinking is a technique which can help us to harness and exercise this strength.

The good news is that Systems Thinking is not complicated to learn. It is relatively simple. But its power, when used properly, is immense.

Mental Models
We store our understanding of the "way things work" in our minds as mental models. These mental models contain everything we have learnt and stored from *all* our past experiences.

For example –
If I press the light switch then the light will come on (cause and effect close together in time);
If I give my horse more food his condition will improve (cause and effect cumulative);
If I plant more fruit tree seeds then I will harvest more apples (cause and effect distant in time).

At this juncture some of you are thinking – that's all very well but that effect may not happen if the trees die before maturity or if I work my horse harder. And of course that is true. In general, the more time distance between cause and effect then the more that other things can get in the way and affect the outcome. For this reason we often have to state the obvious – for example, if I give my horse more food his condition will improve...*all other things being equal* (ie if nothing else changes). We use these "mental models" or "mind maps" on a day to day basis to inform our future courses of action.

People often talk about their mental models as their "point of view". The way I see it is, if we do this, then that will happen. Often people with different points of view will argue and disagree pointedly. Often these disagreements are not resolved and yet it is often the case that both points of view are correct but neither are the full picture. When these mental models are shared and explored we all benefit.

Our mental models are based on all the knowledge we have accumulated in our lives...whether through experience, hear-say, reading, radio, television, school and so on. Some of this is "true" but incomplete. As we saw with the dominoes, "things can look different depending where you stand". We may have some of the pieces of the jigsaw puzzle but not all of them. Sometimes our mental models are further from the truth, by and large due to faulty learning in the past. It is in everyone's interest that we work to improve the quality of our mental models.

The best way to improve our mental models is by making them explicit. Putting them down on paper so that we can challenge, share, analyse, understand and improve them. This is rather like exploring the way our brains are wired and rewiring where necessary to improve the performance of the owner. I believe that we are constantly doing this unconsciously in life but rarely is it done systematically so that learning is acknowledged.

The best way to make our mental models explicit is by using the language of Systems Thinking (ST). There are many excellent texts on this subject (see appendix 1). In this book I will attempt to share the bare bones. The beauty of ST is its simplicity. There are only two basic building blocks; Variables and Relationships.

Variables and Relationships
A **variable** is something that varies (changes in value). It may not be measurable in the normal sense of the word but it must be capable of changing – up and down. For example, the quantity of food my horse eats; the amount of work he does; the condition of my horse; the amount of motivation he has; his acceptance of the bit. These are all variables.

I can measure the quantity of food in a number of ways (weight or in nutritional terms). I can measure the amount of work (quantity and difficulty). I can condition score my horse, weigh him or use a weigh tape. Motivation and acceptance are more difficult to measure objectively but I could measure and monitor it on a subjective scale eg 1 to 10 where 1 means low and 10 means on top of the world.

In contrast "my saddle" or "the weather" are not variables in the Systems Thinking sense of the meaning. They are subjects. However, the "quality of fit of my saddle" is. And the "quality of the weather" is. The weather, whilst being subject to change, is not a specific enough term. We have to ask ourselves what it is about the weather that concerns us. Good examples of weather variables are temperature, or the rainfall or hours of sunshine. These are examples of hard (quantitative) measures of the weather. It is also possible to measure the quality of the weather subjectively on a scale.

> *Do you understand the difference between a variable and a subject?*
> *Can you think of some examples of riding variables?*

Let me get you started: suppleness; straightness; quality of contact; depth of seat; attentiveness; tempo; length of stride; cadence...

> *Take a look at the FEI dressage rules (1). Can you identify more variables?*

Some things take a long period of time to change – they are insensitive. Others change rapidly. Some variables are fixed to all intents and purposes in an individual riding session. *Can you think of examples?*

A **relationship** is a cause and effect connection between two variables. For example, I believe that if I increase the quantity of food the condition of my horse will improve, all other things equal, and vice versa. This is a **Supporting** relationship (the variables move in the **same** direction). It is depicted as an arrow with an **S**.

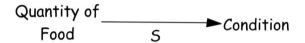

Figure 3 A Supporting relationship

I also believe that if the amount of work increases his condition will go down all other things being equal, and vice versa. This is an **Opposing** relationship (the variables move in the **opposite** direction). It is depicted as an arrow with an **O**.

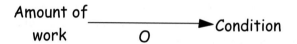

Figure 4 An Opposing relationship

That is it. There are only 2 kinds of relationships. Note that this says nothing about the size of the effect, the shape of the effect, the timeframe and so on. Only that I believe there is an effect in one of two directions. Capturing relationships between variables enables us to make our mental models explicit.

Digging deeper
To explore our understanding more we have to ask ourselves questions. The two most important questions are "What else?" and "How?".
What else affects my horse's condition? I am sure that you can think of many more variables. Eg, temperature, amount of rain, wind-speed, quality of shelter, quality of rugs, grazing time, quality of grazing, time

spent grazing, stress, injury, confinement, illness, worm burden, age, quality of teeth etc. The idea is to think of all things which could have an effect; not just the most important ones.

It is useful to think about what helps to improve the variable (enablers) and what gets in the way or hinders improvement (blockers). We can also ask the question "who?" Who has an interest in this variable? What do they want from it? What must we give in return?

We actively diverge and consider the effects from all angles without judgement. When do I stop? I stop when my thought process starts to dry up. The next steps will often reveal more variables too.

For each of the variables we believe has an impact we now need to understand the direction of the effect. For example, how does temperature affect condition? If temperature goes up what happens to condition all other things equal? For me it is not clear. It could go either way. This means that I have to think about why that is and perhaps introduce extra explanatory variables. On the one hand if temperature increases, more grass will grow and condition will improve. On the other hand, if temperature increases my horse will be more likely to sweat when I work him and so he will lose condition. What happens if temperature decreases? My horse may get cold and shiver, or at least more of his resources will be devoted to keeping him warm, and so his condition will fall.

So expressing this in Systems Thinking terminology gives us:-
Temperature→ (S) Grass→ (S) Condition...overall S
And
Temperature→ (S) Sweating→ (O) Condition...overall O
And
Temperature→ (O) Shivering→ (O) Condition...overall S
NB An even number or no O's means overall an S. An odd number of O's means an overall O.

How does Grass affect Condition? We need to be clearer about what we mean by grass. Grass consumed affects condition. And grass available affects grass consumed.

So,
Temperature→ (S) Grass available→ (S) Grass consumed→ (S) Condition.
But also,
Grass consumed→ (O) Grass available

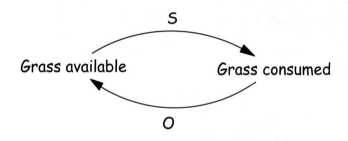

Figure 5 A Feedback Loop

The two variables are inter-related. The posh name for a circle or causal loop of relationships between two or more variables is "feedback".

Feedback
Often our analysis can lead to the identification of feedback. Sometimes this happens quite quickly with only a few or no intermediate variables. For example, X affects Y affects Z affects X. Sometimes this happens very slowly with many intermediate variables and delays. For example, X affects Y affects Z affects A affects B affects C affects D affects E affects…affects X!

In the same way that a chain of relationships can be supporting or opposing so can a feedback loop of relationships. Feedback loops that are supporting are called Reinforcing loops. Feedback loops that are opposing are called Balancing loops. Reinforcing loops reinforce the direction you start with. Balancing loops change the direction you start with.

Reinforcing loops are sources of growth and decline. Their behaviour is exponential. This means that the size of the change doubles each repeat of the cycle. Let's try it...

1, 1x2=2, 2x2=4, 4x2=8, 8x2=16, 16x2=32, 32x2=64, 64x2=128, 128x2=256, 256x2=512, 512x2=1024, 1024x2= 2048, 2048x2= 4096, 4096x2=8192, 16384, 32768, 65536, 131072, 262144, 524288, 1048576 ....

In this example, the initial changes are relatively small but then suddenly huge changes are manifest. If we don't appreciate that a structure like this is at work we could either abandon an activity that is on the way to working or fail to recognise the slow development of a huge problem.

Figure 6 A Thinking Frog

I am told that if you place a live frog in a pan of boiling water he jumps straight out. If, however, you place a live frog in a pan of cold water and bring it slowly to the boil the frog cooks...He becomes the victim of an exponential behaviour pattern that he had not appreciated.

Imagine that I could fold a piece of A4 paper 40 times. It starts off very thin and with an A4 surface area. After one fold the surface area halves and the height doubles. I repeat this folding 40 times. How tall do you think that the paper tower would be?
Answer: The paper tower would reach to the moon as the growth in height is exponential. If you don't believe me get a calculator and work it out for yourself!

Also, I find it incredibly interesting that on the 39th fold I would only be half way there.

In contrast, balancing loops constrain or control growth and decline. They are the source of the statement "nothing grows forever".

Feedback is vital to all systems. Balancing loops, in particular, are a force for equilibrium; they prevent things getting out of control. Biological balancing loops are geared to survival. For example, when it gets too hot I will sweat which in turn cools me down. When we humans wish to control (or manage the performance of) something we design balancing loops. Usually these loops have a variable we want to influence. We set a target value for that variable and we monitor the gap between the actual value and the target. When the actual is below target we take action to improve the actual value. When we are on-target we reward the achievement in some way; this may mean that we simply cease acting!

In practice this is nowhere near as easy as it sounds.

We are juggling with many balancing loops in this way when we ride. Unfortunately we often don't know what we need to work on; what our target should be; how much is too little; how much is too much; how much is just right; when to act.

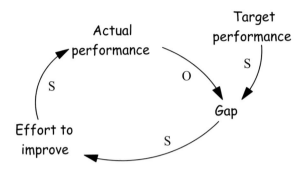

Figure 7 Balancing Loop with Target

Things get even more complicated when there are delays between cause and effect. A good example is when we first try a new shower in a hotel. Perhaps the water is too cold and we turn up the thermostat. There is often a delay before the water temperature adjusts. If we are impatient for our shower, we often push the thermostat up again. It feels just right and we jump in...then seconds later the water is scalding! If we were to carry on in this way and over- react we will see chaotic behaviour in the system. If we understand the delays in the system we will be more cautious with our intervention.

We can often find such effects at work when we ride. And we are juggling with many more ingredients. For example, I feel I need more energy so I pick up my whip and ask for canter. This can give me too much energy and I lose my ability to control it. So I concentrate on quiet work in walk. Perhaps I overdo it and lose my forwardsness again. So I may canter again and so on. I am always trying to find the right balance of ingredients. This requires great self control – both mind and body.

Things get more complicated still when it is not the variable itself but an accumulation of past variables causing the effect. This is the source of our famous saying, "the straw that broke the camel's back". Examples from the horse world include feeding poor quality and/or unsoaked hay or riding on a bad surface. Like the boiled frog we don't see the effect immediately so carry on regardless because we either don't see or choose not to see the structure behind it. Once the horse has COPD it is too late. Once the horse has bad legs it is too late.

Can you think of any other examples which have affected you?

We can view our diagrams either as causal loop diagrams (CLD) or we can rearrange our causal loop diagrams and view them as driver trees. We can select a variable from our CLD and construct a driver tree showing a hierarchy of the variables affecting it. So for example taking the CLD in figure 7 and converting it into a driver tree format for the variable "Actual performance" gives us the following:

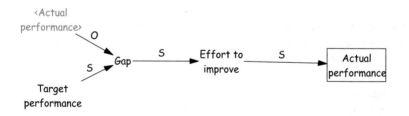

Figure 8 Driver tree

This says actual performance is affected by effort to improve. In turn, effort to improve is affected by the size of the gap. The gap is greater if target performance increases. The gap is smaller as actual performance increases.

Note that Figure 7 (CLD) and Figure 8 (driver tree) are exactly the same. They are just different representations of the same structure.

Some people prefer to work with a CLD and others the linear representation of a driver tree.

In a similar way we can also construct an effects tree of all the variables impacted by a selected variable.

Figure 9 Effects Tree

This says that actual performance affects the size of the gap. As performance increases the gap decreases all other things equal. The size of the gap affects effort to improve. The larger the gap, the greater the effort.

We can view these trees to different levels; from just one level of only the variable directly impacted, to a complete listing of the variables impacted whether directly or indirectly.

We have to think very carefully about **how** the relationships work when we build our diagrams. Quite often effects we think of as direct are actually indirect. Let me give you an example. A class of students is asked what drives milk production. The list they generate includes cows, grass consumed, milk produced by each cow, temperature, health, number of calves and so on.

We then need to ask how does each of these factors affect milk production? It can feel tempting to see them all as direct effects. However, of the list above, only cows and milk per cow have a direct effect. Every other factor works through these to drive milk production. That is to say, they are indirect drivers.

Equilibrium

What is equilibrium? Equilibrium is "no change". It means that everything stays the same, the same, the same. And provided nothing changes it will remain that way.

This means that if we have a state of equilibrium, and we wish to maintain it, we must avoid changing anything. But we all know that things will change. If we are riding the track down the long side of a riding arena we will inevitably have to ride a corner. This is change. The best way to achieve and maintain equilibrium is therefore on a circle. But the surface must be consistent to ensure our circle is unchanging. And it goes without saying that our circle must be truly circular and the horse must be consistently bent. We can then feel for minute changes and act in a minute way to correct them and maintain the equilibrium.

But if we are to ride we must be able to ride through change. Indeed, good transitions are fundamental to our training. We need to be able to manage our equilibrium through turns, over undulating ground, in different paces, in variations of pace within a pace, and through many different exercises in the riding arena.

How can we do this without upsetting the equilibrium? Not changing does not help us to accept change. We must get used to change so we understand how it feels. We must prepare for all changes – and make them as gradual as possible. As we, and our horse, get stronger, we are better able to cope with more immediate (and therefore more demanding) changes.

We often think of balance and equilibrium as similar terms with similar meanings. They are not. Balance is about even-ness – neither too much nor too little. Equilibrium is a state without change. It is possible to achieve equilibrium without balance on horseback but it tends to be either unsustainable or undesirable.

Improvement

Once we have created a satisfactory cause and effect diagram we can use it to inform choices about improvement. There are a number of principles to bear in mind.

First we must address **root causes**. We have already understood the concept of cause and effect driver trees. At the very tips of the branches we find the core enablers – the building blocks that drive everything else. So for example in figure 8 there is only one root cause, "target performance". Root causes can be far removed from the results we are trying to influence. If we choose to ignore root causes any results we do achieve will be illusory and unsustainable.

It can be very tempting to take the easy route with a quick fix. For example, a tight flash noseband will ensure our horse doesn't open his mouth because he can't! This is an easy quick fix in that it treats the symptom but it doesn't treat the cause. Ask yourself, why is the horse opening his mouth in the first place? If it is because of an uncomfortable bit or a problem with his teeth or a rider's insensitive hands the quick fix may mask the symptoms in the short term. In the long term the real cause will wreak havoc elsewhere.

Can you think of any other obvious quick fixes that fail in horsemanship?

Some fixes become addictive. A good example of this is fiddling the horse's head down. This results in a change in the outline but without acceptance in the horse. The minute the rider stops fiddling or holding the horse's head down then the problem immediately resurfaces and so we have to do it more – more fiddling and therefore more strength needed by the rider. The horse's head waggles from side to side or he over-bends; we simply shift the problem elsewhere.

Sometimes we unintentionally escalate a problem and make it far worse than it would otherwise be. I discovered that my Lusitano, Eric, does not like to work in the rain or indeed in a school with surface water splashing on his nose. Of course I can avoid riding outdoors in the rain or ride indoors but sometimes this is not possible. If, as I come towards a puddle, I react by tensing in the expectation of a fight, invariably the fight happens. If, on the other hand, I focus on doing nothing and inhibiting my reaction then there is no fight. He reacts to the puddle but I don't react to him and therefore escalate the problem.

We can react or we can pause to think and choose a different way. It is up to us.

Can you think of any instances where you have reinforced bad behaviours in your horse?

Second, we can only take action within our **sphere of influence**. Some enablers will be within our influence and others will not. Any intervention must be designed around those enablers that are within our sphere of influence. It is pointless and frustrating to try to influence things that are outside our control.

The thing we are most able to change (as it is directly in our sphere of influence) is our own behaviour.

Third, we must understand the **role of time**. How long will it take to change an individual variable? And what about timing? Is there a better or worse time to take action?

Some variables may be changed quite quickly. Others may take a lifetime to change. Usually our ability to influence things increases as we extend the time horizon we consider. When we consider "forever" (infinity), anything is possible. This means that what we can work on in our next hour is necessarily limited. And our focus must always be on the core enablers.

Fourth, we must identify and remove **blockers**. It is pointless pushing on the accelerator with the brakes firmly on. How many times do we see riders complaining about their horse's lack of energy but they are riding with a very strong contact?

Fifth, look for **leverage**. That is the little intervention that makes the big difference. Feedback loops give us leverage. Once we engage a reinforcing loop in a virtuous direction we will continue to reap great benefit...until something changes. We are constantly seeking leverage when we ride our horse. In this instance, leverage is his sensitivity to our requests. We need to find out how little we can do to get a response in the right direction and then aim for less......

To find out "how little" we must be prepared to experiment. And we must be able to start from a position where we are sure we are doing nothing to start with (ie our effect on the total system is passive).

Finally remember that for an action to succeed we must know what to do, how to do it, and why to do it. The existence of this book is a testament to this approach. Consider the following diagram. Have a go at understanding it!

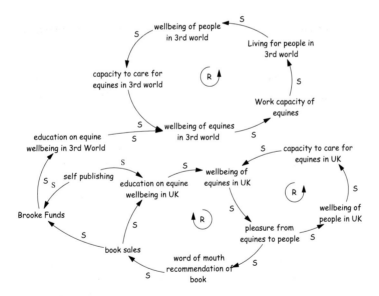

Figure 10 Impact of this book

The diagram captures the cause and effect logic for the existence of the book. You may remember the following words from chapter 1:

"I also wanted to give something back. To whom? To horses and their people. I feel that by sharing this thinking with people like you in the developed world I hope that I can benefit people and horses in the developed world. Equally, by using the book to raise funds for an international horse charity, The Brooke Organisation, I am benefiting equines in less developed countries and therefore the people there who depend on them for their livelihood. And by buying this book you are too."

For more information on Systems Thinking see Peter Senge's "The Fifth Discipline" (26) and Dennis Sherwood's "Seeing the Forest for the Trees" (27). Further resources can be obtained via Pegasus Communications (39).

Things to remember
To achieve a harmonious equilibrium with our horse we must understand the structure of the system.
Structure affects behaviour.
Mental models can be made explicit by using the language of Systems Thinking.
There are only two types of relationships between variables: Supporting and Opposing.
There are only two types of feedback loop: Reinforcing and Balancing.
Reinforcing loops are very powerful and can be vicious or virtuous in their impact.
Driver trees are a linear way of looking at a causal loop diagram.
Equilibrium is a state without change.
We can use Systems Thinking to think through the consequences of our actions and so make better informed choices.

4 Connection in Theory

Good riding is about creating an efficient and effective system (a horse and rider system). In chapter 3 we learnt that sustainable systems are characterised by strong connections. In the following three chapters we learn how to create and strengthen our connection with our horse, enabling us to communicate with him and improve him.

I believe that to achieve improvement we must
Connect (rider to horse; horse to rider) - establish a channel for communication and keep it active;
Communicate (rider to horse and horse to rider) - enabled by maintaining strong connections; and
Comprehend (both horse and rider) – this is the process of training; of discovery and learning about each other. This requires two things; that we comprehend what to communicate and that our horse understands.

In our human world, to have a phone conversation we need to establish a connection before we can communicate. Once we have a connection, then the quality of the connection affects the quality of communication possible.

It is the same with our horse. We need a connection because we can't communicate without it. And the quality of the connection will affect the quality of communication possible. So we need to continually monitor and improve our connection.

Many riders think primarily of connection as being about "contact"; the connection in the hand. However, the biggest surface area of contact is the seat (knee to pelvis). The seat is the most intimate vehicle for communicating with the horse. Because it is "hidden", it gives us the possibility of invisible (and inaudible) communication.

There is an argument that a progression is achieved as the horse's training advances - from voice and whip on the lunge to leg into hand and ultimately to seat. The belief is that the horse becomes lighter and lighter to the hand and leg and then is entirely in the seat and (perhaps later) some telepathic connection. Paul Belasik advocates a progression like this in his "Dressage for the 21st century".(7)

I don't entirely agree with this progression. I prefer the horse to learn to carry himself from the start. This takes longer but the horse never learns to use the rider as a prop. Equally the rider must be careful not to ask for more than the horse can do without leaning on the hand.

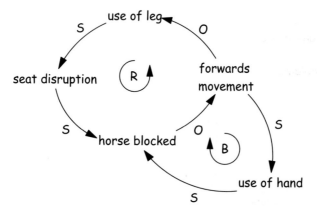

Figure 11 Leg and Hand

All my life I have searched for the secret recipe; the Holy Grail of riding. Little did I know that it was always there inside me. So, deep breath, here's the secret. **The ingredients for successful riding are the same ingredients for success in any aspect of life.** The only difference is the quantity of each ingredient required and the way that we choose to mix those ingredients.

Creating a quality connection can be likened to baking a cake. I believe that there are two key mixtures in the recipe for our connection cake:
    (1)   The rider's ability to connect to the horse and
    (2)   The horse's ability to connect to the rider.

Each mixture is made from three other basic ingredients. For the rider, they are calmness, concentration and mind-body connection. For the horse, they are calmness, concentration and mind-body connection. The same things!

The rider is the chef. She decides to ride the horse so she must be in charge of the ingredients. Unfortunately, her ability to influence the horse's ingredients *directly* is limited. Instead she must focus on improving her ability to connect to the horse, which in turn means that she has to work on her own three ingredients. As the connection improves she can start to work on the horse's ingredients. But she must always be conscious of monitoring, retaining and improving her own.

Rider Ingredients

The first two ingredients for the rider are calmness and concentration. We all lead busy lives with busy brains. We always need to be somewhere else. We are always planning. Our attention is constantly demanded outside ourselves. We worry and send our minds into a writhing turmoil. At times my mind feels like it could burst. My thoughts can be like a raging storm in a sea and I feel tossed about by them. At such times my horse becomes just another commitment – another test – and then I must be somewhere else.

How can I expect it to work? I want him to give me his undivided attention but I don't give him mine. The frustration I feel leads to ever more stormy seas.

This is not a good way forward. We must learn to control ourselves. We must calm our mind, still the stormy waters and focus our attention on the inside of our self and our horse. If we can't do this we can't expect harmony in our training. We must do something different instead.

How can we achieve this? Constant attention. Little by little.

What helps you to feel calm? What gets in the way? For me, meditation, focus on my breathing and positive thinking have a positive impact; whilst pressure, distractions, teacher's shouting, "friends" watching, lacking time and feeling rushed are negative. To improve our calmness and concentration we must use the things that help (the enablers) and mitigate the things that get in the way (the blockers).

Working on the enablers means that we must let go of the need to "get him round" and the temptations that this will create for a quick fix (fiddling the reins and so on). Instead, we don't care what our horse does, within limits, as we focus on breathing and softening ourselves. Feeling where we are holding on (muscle tension) and letting go...allowing the movement into us rather than resisting it. Trot, with it's regular 2-beat, is an ideal pace for warming both of you up in this way.

Mitigating the effect of the blockers is a skill that we need to learn. We can block physically or mentally. The physical side means that I must control my environment (for example, by riding in an indoor school with no-one else present). The mental side means that I must control myself. It is not always possible to control our environment so we must continually work on controlling ourselves.

Do you remember those "snow scene" toys you played with as a child? You shake them and the snow is everywhere, blotting out the scene in front of you. If we let go and set the toy down the snow eventually settles and things become calmer and clearer in the scene. This is what we need to do with our minds. Only when calmness has been achieved can we start to feel. It is the same for our horse.

What we are aiming for here is an easy equilibrium in our newly formed horse and rider system. It is a quiet, effortless place where horse and rider have achieved a sustainable balance. Neither horse nor rider are affecting each other negatively or positively. We are "doing nothing". Indicators that we have achieved this with the horse include a regular rhythm and relaxation of the horse's frame, resulting in stretching forwards and down, and relaxed snorting. When this happens I know I am going in the right direction.

It is my belief that each time we get on our horse we have to (a) re-establish the connections and (b) get to the point of "doing nothing" with ease, before we can start to "do something".

A calm, concentrated mind enables us to get in touch with our body. To feel areas of tension and to let go, thereby achieving a more balanced and connected posture. This is our third rider ingredient; the mind-body connection.

We expect our horses to be supple and straight but what about us? Slumping in a chair in front of our computer for eight hours a day is not great preparation for riding. The strength of connection necessary for our horse to graze, or for us to work away at our computer, are much less than for harmonious riding. Poor posture at the computer is not good for us either but the impact is less obvious than when we ride. Cause and effect are distant and cumulative and so, like the boiled frog, we often don't notice until it is too late.

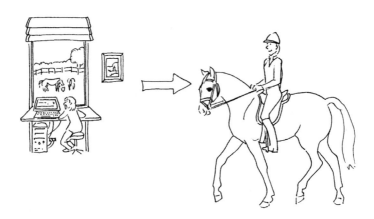

Figure 12 Before and after

We can't have free limbs without alignment in our spine and we can't have this without a stable pelvis and we can't have this without core strength. And we can't use our core strength if we have tension.

The rider must take responsibility for her own weight. She must minimise the burden of her own weight on the horse. She must come into self-carriage before her horse can. She must organise her body to achieve this and then her FULL-TIME JOB is to continually monitor and intervene when necessary to re-align and soften her self.

To do this she needs to be capable of controlling each muscle in her body and the degree of tension therein. She needs to develop a feel for how much tension is necessary, and where. What is superfluous? What is inhibiting? And release...release...release any excess.

There is a lot of talk about relaxation in the horse world. But I believe that the word is misleading as it conjures up images of lying around on a sofa or in bed. It goes without saying that we don't want tension. We want that middle point where things are at their natural length but no more than that. Take an elastic band and just hold it at each side. That is total relaxation. Now pull the two ends until the band is tight. This is tension. Now move your fingers until the band is just straight. There is no tension – but no total relaxation either.

Relaxation is a variable. At one end of the scale we have tension and stiffness and at the other we have wobbly jelly! In the middle we have our desired state. The Alexander Technique and Pilates are two regimes that can help you to achieve this state. Both are discussed in chapter 8.

Notice that the first three ingredients (calmness, concentration and connection) only involve the rider, so we can start to work on them before we mount our horse. Once we have chosen to put ourselves on his back we have a duty to minimise the burden he carries and to establish a connection with him that enables us to achieve our purpose in riding.

Strengthening the connection

The horse is a system. The human is a system. When the human attempts to ride the horse she endeavours to create a new system – a horse and rider system. The harmony and strength of this system is based on its connectedness. The stronger the connection, the more harmony, the more the appearance of something greater than the sum of the parts. The weaker the connection, the less harmony. It becomes only the sum of the parts or even less.

Developing the connection is complex and involves us carrying on with work on ourselves (the rider ingredients) and also working on the horse. The horse needs to have the same ingredients as the rider ie calmness, concentration, connectedness of his mind-body. A horse that has too much or too little of any of the necessary ingredients is difficult to connect with.

The connection is something we feel, not hear or see. Often the connection is relative. Do we feel more or less connected with the horse than we did two minutes ago? The connection can always be improved. It must be attended to constantly.

To improve the strength of the connection we need to identify the "ingredients" that we currently have too much or too little of and work out how to rectify the balance. The interesting thing is that unlike baking where we start with an empty bowl, in riding we start with two bowls which already have a certain amount of each ingredient present – those of the rider and those of the horse.

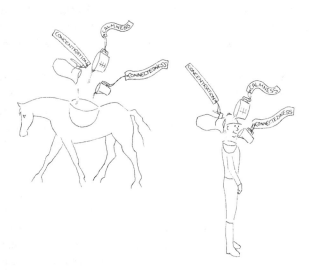

Figure 13 Horse and Rider Mixing Bowls

A new cook will follow a recipe to the letter. Carefully weighing precisely the right ingredients and adding them in precisely the right sequence. As confidence grows the more experienced chef will experiment with ingredients, sequencing and so on. The really confident chef will create their own personal recipes, often by adapting existing basic ones.

We follow the same progression in our riding. However, unlike baking, the novice rider can't have her riding recipe book open in front of her when she rides!

Influencing the horse's ingredients

We need to understand what we have now, what we need to have and how to move towards the desired state. This means that first of all we need to assess how much of each ingredient we currently have in our horse mixing bowl. How calm is he? How much share of his mind do I have? How connected and coordinated is his movement?

The horse does the work in riding; the rider develops him so that the work becomes easier. By training his mind and his body, she helps him to understand what she requires, she builds his strength and flexibility and she stays out of his way and lets him get on with it.

To calm and relax him we have to build his trust in us. We engage his brain and, focus it on us and his work, rather than the scarey monster in the corner of the school, or his friends in the field. We must arrange his body, as we have ours, so that his back is aligned and strong, his pelvis is engaged and his limbs are free. Before all of this, though, we have to calm, concentrate and collect ourselves to a greater degree than the horse. This is a guiding principle in all our work with the horse – be first what you want your horse to be.

Naturally there are different degrees of calmness, concentration and collection necessary for different activities. For example, lower degrees are required for hacking than for Grand Prix dressage. But there will always be instances where the hacker will need all the C's of the Grand Prix rider, for example, when a bus is approaching and the horses in the field to your left are playing tag, and vice versa.

We know we are achieving our goal when the connection we have with the horse gets stronger.

How can we influence the level of these ingredients in the horse? We can use our Systems Thinking to understand what helps and what hinders each ingredient.

Let's start with calmness.

> *What affects your horse's calmness?*

Some things I have found to have an impact are:
- My calmness
- Spookiness of environment
- Wind speed
- Familiarity with the work
- Difficulty of the work
- Horse's confidence that "he is doing it right"
- Consistency of the approach
- Time since the horse was last ridden
- Time horse has spent in field
- ...the list goes on.

> *How does each of these variables affect calmness?*
> *What other variables do they affect?*

All of these things are "chicken and egg"...they are mutually reinforcing. So, the calmer I am, the calmer my horse is likely to be, and the calmer my horse is, the calmer I will be. And vice versa. The source of increasing calmness or increasing anxiety (tension) is the same reinforcing loop. We choose to ride the horse, so first and foremost we have a duty to be calm.

Note that the less calm the horse, the more need for the rider to be calm, in order to avoid reinforcing the horse's anxiety.

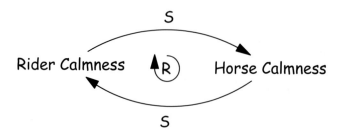

Figure 14 R loop Calmness

After we have become sufficiently calm, we must help our horse to be calm. If he is already calm we can commence with simple easy work looking after the rhythm and speed. If he is anxious, we must ensure we don't reinforce this anxiety. We can help him to calm him by giving him other things to focus on, such as more difficult movements.

It is good to lunge our horse before we ride him. In this way we get to assess his ingredients before we burden him with our weight.

What about concentration? What affects that?

Some examples include:
- Rider concentration
- Spookiness of environment
- Familiarity of the work (Note that here the effect is in the opposite direction. That is to say, familiarity reinforces calmness but perhaps decreases attention, as the horse doesn't have to concentrate so much if he finds the work easy)
- Something to pay attention to – movements, transitions etc

When I have the connection I desire it feels like the horse is seeking to carry me. He feels comfortable and easy to sit on. His back feels strong under me – seeking contact with the whole of my seat. His sides feel pushed out seeking contact with my legs. His neck and ears stretch away from me and he seeks a gentle contact with my hand via the reins. When the mix of ingredients is right all horses do this.

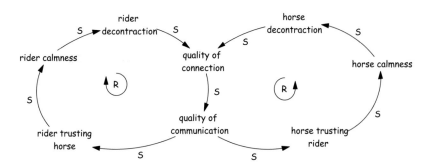

Figure 15 Reinforcing (R) loop connection and communication

Things to remember
To create a strong system we must strengthen the connections.
Connection is something we feel.
The rider's role is to unblock not to block.
The key rider ingredients are calmness, concentration and connectedness.
The key horse ingredients are calmness, concentration and connectedness.
The rider must control her own ingredients before she can influence those of her horse.

5 Connection in Practice

So that's the theory. But what actually happens in practice? The connection to the horse is both mental and physical. Let's start with the physical connection. We make physical contact with the horse with our hand, our seat and our leg.

Hands
The first point of contact I want to consider is the connection between the rider's hand and the horse's head. I originally wrote the word "bit", rather than head, but then it occurred to me that some riders use a bit-less bridle and we lunge from a cavesson - so bits are not always involved in this connection.

Which raises the question, do we have to use a bit? If we don't compete in dressage the answer is "no". If you do compete in dressage, however, the rules require that you must use a bit. In particular, the FEI rules require the horse to be "on the bit". This means that *"...he accepts the bridle with a light and soft contact..."* (1)

This raises more questions than it answers!
What is contact?
When do we cross the line between having and not having a contact?
How light is "light"?
When is the contact said to become hard?
How do I know the horse has accepted the bridle?
What affects acceptance? Lightness? Softness? Contact?

What is contact?
The Official Instruction Handbook of the German National Equestrian Federation states "Contact is the soft, steady connection between the rider's hand and horse's mouth". *(6)*

Is a consistent (steady) connection with a loop in the rein still a contact? The German National Equestrian Federation requires that the horse "'seek' a contact with the rider's hand, thus 'going onto' the contact" *(6)*

When do we cross the line between seeking and not seeking a contact?
Can we have contact with a loop in the rein?
Is it desirable to have a loop in the rein?

I sought the views of today's dressage judges and trainers in my survey.
I asked:-
"How would you judge a rider who rode her horse and did all the test
movements perfectly - her horse is truly engaged behind and in a
beautiful outline in front (light and easy on the forehand; loose through
the shoulders; soft in the neck) where the reins are like a thread of silk
(the picture I am thinking of is Nuno Oliveira - the reins *just* slack. See
photos in "Reflections on Equestrian Art".) - BUT a slight loop always in
the reins. What collective marks and comments would you give?"

There were a vast range of opinions, even amongst judges of the same
level. All of these responses were received via email, which has
influenced the written style of some of the respondents.

"As we are discussing competition I would have to say under **submission**:
'needs to develop a more secure connection from hindquarters into the
contact'. I could not give more than a **6**.
Whilst the image you are describing is desirable under certain schools
of thought (particularly the Iberian) it would not be viewed so under
FEI definitions that require the horse to make a **secure contact** (note –
the horse, not the rider). The above would be viewed as a horse hanging
slightly behind the contact, for whatever reason."
*****
"Rider mark of **8 or 9**. I agree - threads of silk are the ideal – but
there has to be a **soft, elastic connection** so the lightest of aids can be
delivered and utilised to best effect – and a loop in the reins may mean a
delay in the aid being received and acted upon – if that were the case
then marks through the test might be one mark below expectation. "
*****
"This isn't an answerable question! I'm not dodging the issue. The
reason I say this is that you cannot compare **classical** dressage concepts
with **competitive** dressage parameters. They are two entirely different
ball games – **they should not be, but they are**!"

"This has never happened to me – at least not all of it, all together, in one combination. However, if such an apparition presented itself – then **9's and 10's are there for the giving**. Collective marks would be similarly high. Comments would be short and to the point – '**a pleasure to judge. How refreshing to see such a harmonious partnership**'. I would probably feel the need to congratulate the rider at the end of their test.
Contact is not solely about the tautness, or otherwise, of the rein. It is much deeper and broader than that; it's about the connection and throughness."

*****

"Dressage is about harmony and if the picture was of harmony in a partnership then I would be glad to give **high marks**"

*****

"Almost impossible to answer without seeing the test. Provided there was some contact, however slight, the marks would be extremely high. If there was <u>no</u> contact, then marks would be deducted under 'submission' and 'rider' with a possible comment of 'horse work through back and take contact' or something similar."

*****

"With riders I've seen that are in photos with a loop, **in real time they have loop/snatch/loop/snatch**, so I'm not necessarily impressed by that."

*****

"Would depend on the level the horse is working at but would advise that they **maintain a steady even contact at all times, so the horse feels secure**"

*****

"The loop in the reins: for a true modern dressage test at lower levels, **the horse would be deemed not into the rein**. This is really more for training, and if the horse is in self carriage and has ease of the movements then I would not judge it harshly, but bear in mind that the collectives have a part on submission for acceptance of the bridle. **We are taught that the horse that truly works over the back will do so into the rein.** I think it is really the rider who will create the contact in return. Some of my horses are much lighter with a more advanced degree of collection and of course you can test for self carriage with a give and retake. As a rider I would always say that a horse who is truly working correctly can be identified by how they react in a spook. **One working correctly will spook into the rein and seek the contact... not draw back away from it.** "

*****

"I would be watching to see whether the horse was elastic and whether it stayed in balance in transitions (particularly within the paces) as a light elastic contact is usually needed for this and the horse should be seeking a light contact with the rider in order to work over his back. The collective marks would depend on the quality of the test. "

*****

"I would be happy to give **very good marks** but I would comment that **I would like to see a more positive connection between the hand and the bit.**"

*****

"8/9's but not often seen. So often see tension. "

*****

"If the horse is in carriage, supple, elastic then I think a given rein is acceptable but **to actually ride a test like that is probably not possible** because when you are having to do a series of advanced movements in quick succession I think that the contact could be extremely light but you would probably not see a slight loop in the reins."

*****

"I have not seen the picture but on what you describe – the attributes of the scales of training are nearly all there, **except Contact.** I would probably have to **deduct 1 mark from each** of the collectives because I think **the horse is slightly 'holding' itself and not truly 'through' to a light (non restrictive) contact.**
Paces - would underline freedom – is it truly free?
Imp – could it go more forwards – to contact?
Submission – is it not happy to take a contact?
Rider – not riding enough to contact "

*****

"Depends on whether the horse takes his nose forward, pushes (not just engaged) from behind and swings through his back as required. If this can be achieved with just the "weight of the reins" as contact then it's OK. The horse is then "to " the contact. It is difficult though to indicate to the horse to go more outward (stretch) and forward with this flimsy contact, so one is left with judging and commenting on the result, that **the horse is seen to be off/behind the contact when asked to lengthen. It is often used as an excuse for having the horse off and behind the contact.** You and the horse need to clearly understand the two concepts of holding position when the contact is yielded, and taking the rein forward (and down), and the horse to be able to do either on request and without locking his back. "

*****

"As a judge if the movements were perfect then she would be scoring **9 and 10's** throughout the test then the collectives would have to reflect this, but a loop in the rein would probably indicate that the horse was holding himself with some tension in the neck and **not necessarily working forward into the contact** so this would be in the comment. The **submission mark would be affected** as would the rider mark. Impossible to say fairly here without seeing the whole test!"

*****

"My view is that this is acceptable to show that the horse is in self carriage by momentarily giving the reins, but would want to see true contact restored and the horse seeking the bit. My collective mark would be 9 if the contact was not sought after and 10 if it was then restored. My comment for 9 would be – Very good, but would like to see a consistent contact – horse seeking the bit

My comment for 10 would be – Very good! A goose-bump moment!!"

*****

"Fantastic – an example of true self carriage and stunning to watch. Should receive very high marks."

*****

"**10s all round** because you say it is perfect! An absolute pleasure to watch and judge I can now retire!"

*****

"To get to the root of this question...,there is a problem here because few are capable of riding like Nuno Oliveira and to get the same effect they resort to using strong bits, nerve points, pulleys etc and the result is the opposite of what I think you are aiming at...a happy horse ridden in a natural way. The thing about Nuno Oliveira was that he rode with a definite contact even though it was very light..., I believe that to teach this it is necessary to first get the rider to have a normal contact going with the movement of the horse's mouth. To start with a lighter contact than this is more difficult for most riders. This type of contact is also only possible with an ability to use very small aids and with a horse that is between the aids and through the back. Regarding the dressage test I believe the rules demand a 'normal' rein contact therefore this is what is required during the test.

As the rider gets more in harmony and the horse improves physically and the mental relationship improves it is possible to have an extraordinarily light contact...our aim...but also a very definite contact. It is the touch of a good lover. The judge knows because signs of unhappiness and unnaturalness are obvious...with a good experienced judge!"

*****

"For the test you describe, as a Judge I would be in heaven. Most likely my main emotion would be **envy** - I would love to ride like that! But to see such a vision of quality with the most tentative rein connection is the 'other side of perfection', in that **you can go too far in minimising the contact**... Your question seems to focus on the slight loop in the reins. A slight loop, maintained at all times, indicates to me that the **rider is following the movement of the poll, face, jaw and mouth with an exquisite touch and sensitivity.** This is not possible without sitting centrally and in superb balance... Collectives:

P - (Can't be sure, but if the movements were executed perfectly...) perhaps 8

I - (Engaged behind, carrying the weight to release the shoulder) 8

S - (Following the rider's wishes from the most minimal aids) 9

R - (Demonstrating balance and sensitivity) 9

Comments:

"A wonderful demonstration of harmony and partnership. Horse shows lightness and agility and a desire to please. However, would like to see more obvious connection from hand to bit with the horse drawing forward to the contact, enhancing control of the longitudinal flexion. **It was a privilege to judge this test."**

OK, you've seen some other opinions now what do you think? And why?

Oliveira, in his "Reflections on Equestrian Art" (8), points out that "...it is only by allowing horses to move on a free rein, and not in holding them in, that success may be obtained. Riders who hold in their horses are insignificant riders and will never advance. Riders who give their horses freedom are those who will taste the delicacies of equestrian art".

Mary Wanless in her "Ride with your Mind Essentials" (9) states that "When the reins are loopy, the horse is always 'unstuffed'...".

Do you agree?

Let's start with some pictures. If you get the chance, take a look at Nuno Oliveira in Michel Henriquets book (10); and Klaus Ferdinand Hempfling in his "Dancing with Horses" (19). Or how about Nadine Cappellman in William Micklem's book (5). Do you agree with me that the reins have a loop but the horses are most certainly performing and most certainly are not "unstuffed"?

The best Western Riding and Bull-fighting is always on a loop.

So what is happening here? I think that Mary Wanless is right, that a lot of horses ridden on loopy reins (ie reins that are too long, and often held inconsistently) are unstuffed. But I think that the loop is only a symptom; the root cause lies elsewhere. It is in the whole of the rider.

What makes my horse turn or bend?
I think it is my body, not my hand. My hand only receives and limits the bending and flexion.

What creates forwards movement?
I think it is my body not my hand. My hand only receives and limits the speed. And then only if my body has failed in its ability to do this or my horse has ignored my body aids.

Try this exercise on horseback. Change the length of stride in the walk using only your seat. Restrict the movement in your seat (hold with the seat – not the hand – give the hand forwards) and then let the walk back out again by releasing the seat. As you do this really think of the letting go feeling in the body. Notice what happens to the horse's head and neck. And you didn't use your hands... *What did you learn?*

This happens because the horse has to adjust his balance to walk with shorter steps. The horse uses his head and neck to maintain his balance. This demonstrates the importance of riding from your seat first and just receiving what you create in the hand. When the opposite happens the horse feels blocked and will resist.

This leads me to believe that the term, "On the bit", is misleading at best and downright destructive at worst. I believe that the key connection is from the seat to the hind legs when riding, and from brain to brain in work on the ground eg lunging.

Indeed, the horse's frame matters, but we don't need a connection from hand to mouth to "prove" this. Therefore I prefer the term "connected". And the ultimate connection is independent of the rein.

If we are trying to do work that requires higher levels of strength or suppleness or balance than the horse is currently capable of then the horse will seek support in the hand. It is my belief that if the horse has been taught that putting weight in the rein is acceptable then he will continue to do it. We reap what we sow! So my belief is that we should operate on the boundaries of the horse's self carriage – short pieces of work – frequent rewards – building up ability slowly and solidly and accept that sustainable development takes time.

If we support we build dependence. This is the quick fix that fails in the longer term.

How much tension is needed in the rein?
Mary Wanless describes this in her "Ride with your Mind Essentials" (9) as "There is very little weight in the ends of the reins, but the rider can feel the horse and the horse can feel the rider on a consistent basis."

Contact implies a tension in the rein. But as soon as there is tension there is blocking of forward movement or an over-bent horse. Better to take up a suitable length of rein (so called semi-tension); ensure soft arms (oil your joints) then use your seat and movements to encourage the horse to carry himself with the lightest contact. The horse seeks a contact with the hand and the rider provides it, not the other way around. And always with a forwards thinking allowing hand.

Behind the vertical (BTV)

BTV describes the appearance of the horse's outline through the head and neck. Imagine a piece of string with a stone fastened to the horse's poll (that's the bit in-between the ears). Gravity will ensure that this "plumb line" hangs straight (perpendicular) to the ground. The horse's nose should be on or in front of this line to avoid being behind the vertical irrespective of the height of the head. This means that in Figure 16 the horse on the top left is in front of the vertical. The horse on the top right is behind the vertical. The horse on the bottom centre is on the vertical. In an ideal world I would like to see a horse a little in advance of the vertical with the poll higher.

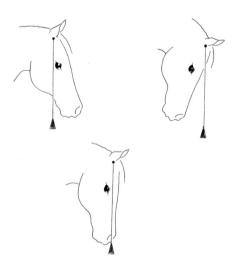

Figure 16 The Vertical

Is it ever acceptable for a horse to be BTV? Some trainers intentionally over-bend their horses outside the competition arena in the practice of "rollkur" or hyperflexion.

> *What do you think?*
> *Is it ever ok for the horse to be above the bit?*
> *Which is the worse fault – above the bit or over bent?*

How light is light?
I think that the answer is simple – only the weight of the rein. In other words the horse doesn't feel any direct force from the rider, he simply feels the weight of the rein. This is comfortable for the rider, and for the horse.

Now for the science. I hated Physics and gave it up before O level. Good job my partner is a physicist and could explain the theory of Newtonian mechanics to me!

When we connect the rein to a bit at one end and the rider's hand at the other we have the possibility of various forces affecting the shape of the rein – gravity (downwards); the weight of the horses head and neck (downwards); and, a balancing force attributable to the rider's arms. An even greater force can be executed by horse or rider, for example, when the horse attempts to lean on the bit or falls against the rein and the same for the rider. Some riders can be seen to use the reins as a water skier would use the rope.

Assume a semi-tension in shortened reins (ie only enough rein and tension for a soft line from bit to hand), thus minimising the effect of gravity on the rein. Assume also no tension in the rein resulting from the horse's head or rider's arm, then the rider/horse connection is in equilibrium. Equilibrium is important as it minimises the force of the horse on the rider and that of the rider on the horse.

In Figure 17 the horse wearing a bridle without any reins feels no weight from the rein as there are no reins. If we attach a pair of reins as in the picture on the bottom left then he begins to feel a small amount of weight on the bit. Adding a rider holding the reins on the buckle, as in the picture on the top right, makes very little difference to the weight the horse feels. Assuming the rider on the bottom right is holding the reins in equilibrium then the horse will feel the least amount of weight possible in the rein (even less than the previous pictures without a contact).

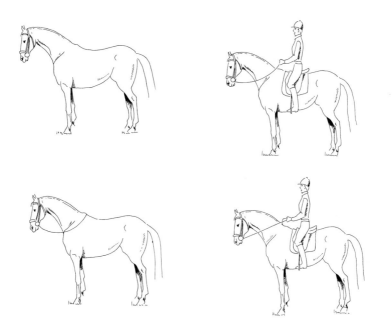

Figure 17 The impact of the reins

What does this feel like in practice?
I weighed an ordinary 5/8" pair of plain leather reins (125 cms in length). They weighed 4 ounces (100 grams) in each rein. So 4 ounces (weight of rein) x 2/3(portion of the rein which is "active" between bit and hand) x $\frac{1}{2}$ (portion of weight in rider's hand) = 1.33 ounces. This is a lot less than the "bag of sugar" advised in some books!

This equilibrium will remain so long as a straight line is maintained from the elbow to the hand to the bit and neither horse or rider introduce any additional force. If the straight line is broken or additional forces are introduced then this equilibrium cannot be maintained.

The straight line and/or the forces may be altered by the rider or by the horse. Let's look at the horse first. The horse can break the straight line by moving his head up or down and he can change the force by moving his mouth backwards or forwards. If he moves his mouth backwards if nothing else changes he will be behind the bit and he will introduce a loop in the rein. The rider feels a non-existent contact. If he moves his mouth forwards (ie leans into the rein) the tension in the rein will increase. The rider feels a great weight in the rein, pulling on her. The horse can move his head up or down either seeking to introduce more or less weight in the rein.

Often at this point instinct intervenes. The rider counteracts weight with weight and a pulling match ensues. Or she rides around proudly revelling in the "lightness" of her riding.

In all cases the rider must adjust her arm to maintain the straight line. She must remove the loop if the horse created it. How? By recreating semi-tension in the rein and sending the horse forwards to the contact and rebalancing as necessary. She must diagnose the cause of the increased weight. If it is a temporary loss of balance then rebalance. If it is a more persistent evasion then the rider must not collude and support and pull herself.

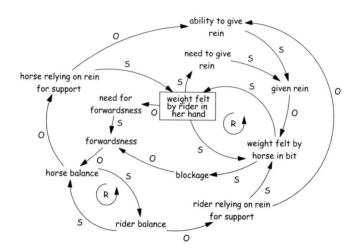

Figure 18 Rebalancing horse and rider

The rider should never create tension in the rein. She should maintain the straight line. If she decides to introduce a loop she needs to differentiate in her seat whether the outline is to be maintained with the loop or whether the horse is expected to remove the loop by seeking the contact at a different point (longer, lower).

I don't admire the rider who can only ride on the loop or the rider with 2lbs in each hand. I believe that a clever rider should be able to choose the contact she desires and keep the horse in a good form. I believe that an ability to work with different degrees of tension in the rein proves everything. However, others do not.

Having considered all the evidence my opinion is that riding with different outlines, with and without a loop in the rein, is NOT better or worse; just DIFFERENT. Believe me doing any of them well is challenging! But the challenges are different...

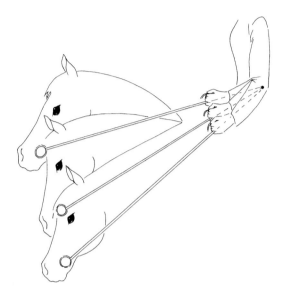

Figure 19 Connection: Hand to Bit

One thing I am clear about is that **an imaginary straight line (from bit to hand to elbow) must be maintained at all times** – if the horse raises his head the hand must rise and if he lowers his head the hand must lower (not vice versa as often seen). This is the same irrespective of the tension in the rein. The rider must understand the dynamics affecting the contact and then use this understanding to influence it to achievable desirable ends. The key here is once again understanding what needs to be done, knowing why it should be done in this way and having the ability to do it.

A loop in the rein introduces the effect of gravity to the weight in the rein. When the rider's hand is higher than the straight line from bit to elbow or advanced on the same straight line towards the bit then the distribution of rein weight between rider and horse changes. It is no longer equal. The horse feels more or less contact, not the ideal "equilibrium" contact.

Interestingly a loop in the rein gives more freedom to the horse but unexpectedly more weight in the bit. When a loop is introduced into the rein by the rider, the horse will seek to remove it to re-equalise the weight distribution. And so minimise the forces he is feeling on the bit. Forwardsness, straightness and balance must be maintained for this to happen.

Differentiating between stretching and maintaining outline in a give & retake (G&R) then becomes clear. For stretching the hand must move along the straight line towards the bit. This means that the angle at the elbow must open. The rider reinforces this with a lighter seat to match the new centre of gravity (figure 20). For G&R the hand moves forwards up the neck. There is no change to the seat (figure 20 bottom right).

Figure 20 Stretching vs G&R

The same principles apply when we lunge our horse. The horse will seek an equilibrium contact on the lunge rein. This means that if we give the rein he will seek to remove the loop by either making the circle larger or by stretching down. The same applies with side reins. Longer side reins encourage a longer outline as the horse seeks to create an equilibrium contact.

Creating a contact
One mental model of riding requires the horse to accept and work between the rider's leg and hand. In this context a half halt is something the rider does to the horse to regain acceptance of the hand. She introduces a degree of non-allowing until the horse gives in.

My mental model is different. I feel that the horse will come into my hand when I am in balance and connected to him through my seat. I do not restrict or attempt to control the front end. I would sooner start with the horse moving freely as we both warm up. When he starts to show signals that he is ready to work I move on. When the horse feels restriction he rebels. The feeling of restriction relates to many things but in particular his ability to do things. For example, my old horse, Shantie, has weak conformation and disability to contend with. For me a half halt is something I do to myself to rebalance myself and reconnect my seat to the horse. It is a "giving" not a non-allowing activity.

What does a half halt mean to you?

Tight or light? In between there are many varying degrees of contact. The contact that is right for one partnership will not be right for another. And the optimal contact for that partnership at a point in time will change too. Like everything else in our riding I believe that our contact is personal. But if you compete you must be seen to have a consistent contact.

The contact is the ultimate performance indicator. It will be "right" when everything else is "right". The big problem with this is that when it is "wrong" you cannot influence it directly. So I believe that we don't work "on the contact". Instead we work on *what affects the contact.*

The Quality of the Contact is a variable; it can get better or worse. It gets better when it is steadier, more even (left to right) and softer.

What affects steadiness? Steadiness of the rider's hands is vital. Consistency (no sudden changes) also matters. This means that we need to establish a rhythm and prepare for all changes (of direction, of pace, of pattern etc) to smooth them. Calmness is essential to consistency.

What affects evenness? Evenness of the riders' hands is vital. Straightness of the horse also affects evenness. Straightness is in turn affected by suppleness (the horse is equally flexible on both sides of his body). Lateral (side to side) balance also plays a key role here.

What affects softness? Softness of the riders' hands is vital. The quality of the horse's balance is key, both lateral and longitudinal (nose to tail). Also the relaxation of the horse's musculature and his free forwards movement.

Do you agree? What do you think?

The common factor in all of these is how acceptable the rider's hand is to the horse. Good hands are even (ie same left and right), light (ie grammes rather than kilos), soft/elastic (no tension in arms and shoulders), quiet (steady connection – hands not moving about) and consistent (like our rhythm = the same, the same, the same).

Creating an acceptable hand

In the learning phase it is essential that our hand is acceptable. An acceptable hand is a forwards thinking hand on the end of a relaxed arm.

A softer feel in the hand may be achieved by twisting the lower arm outward from the wrist. This can be useful for the inside hand in movements such as circles and shoulder in. It is easier to have still hands in trot as there is less movement of the horse's head and neck to accommodate.

We need to develop a hand that our horse can trust and accept. Still hands imply a degree of fixedness and there is nothing fixed about a pair of good hands. Better words would be light and steady. We are told to carry our hands but what does that mean? I think that it means that we need to take responsibility for the weight of our hands and not use the horse's mouth for this purpose.

In my experience there is a lot of rubbish talked about hands. At different times I've been told:
- To have the hands together
- To have the hands at the same level
- To have the fingers mobile
- To close the fingers and soften the wrist
- To ride "from my elbows"
- To introduce a degree of non-allowing in my hand
- To have my hands wider apart for a novice horse to provide "a wider roadway for him to pass through";
- To have my hands low and fixed like side-reins
- To take up more contact. "Give him a contact...he will thank you for that"
- To have the outside hand higher than the inside (see Michel Henriquet (10))
- To have the inside hand higher than the outside (see Heather Moffett (11))
- To give and take with the hand
- To take and hold until the horse gives
- To squeeze the fingers like a sponge
- To close the fingers

Bewildering and conflicting advice! This is all very confusing. What is the right way? The answer could be any of these. We must understand the likely impact of our actions on the 'system'. Think it through. If it makes sense, then try it. Notice what happens. Learn from it. Work out what works for you and your horse.

> *Take a look at rider's hands in photographs in Equitation books.*
> *Which do you like? Why?*
> *Which don't you like? Why?*
> *Ask your friends what they think and why.*

I am drawn to pictures of Nuno Olivera in Reflections on Equestrian Art (8) and Paul Belasik riding Exelso in Dressage for the 21st century (7).

You can only have a forwards thinking hand when you have a soft relaxed arm and shoulders and you can only get this when you have a balanced posture. A balanced posture requires a supportive seat. So to work on our hands, I believe we must first work on our seat.

Without a good seat, the horse still feels the tight arm on a loose rein and is unlikely to seek the contact this will provide – so if we push our tight arms forward the horse is unlikely to stretch down.

The horse will seek the contact when the seat is correct and the arm is relaxed. At this point ensure your reins are short enough so that you can carry your hands out in front of you and never need to bring your hand back or down. Only use hand forwards and up, never back or down. As the horse becomes more collected and up in front you will need to adjust your reins to the new frame. THIS IS ALL VERY DIFFICULT – human instinct is to hold on and control with the hands and we have to "unlearn" this habitual response to progress with our riding.

When our horse hollows it can feel right to take a hold with the reins and "fiddle his head back down". When we feel compelled to do this we must inhibit ourselves and do something very different. We must release in our body, give with the rein. Time after time I know that this works but sometimes I still catch myself desperate for a quick fiddle; old habits die hard!

The time we are most likely to get caught out is when we make a transition from work on a longer rein (eg free walk on a long rein or stretching in trot or canter) to an uphill test outline (poll the highest point). Many riders simply see this as an exercise in shortening the reins (hauling in the front end). This always causes a "fight" as the horse feels the restriction in front. Instead the rider must bring the horse's head up first with her seat. This creates a loop in the rein which the rider can then remove by shortening her reins. The action in the seat goes from passive (following) to controlling (restricting)...but for this to work the rider must have a seat capable of making this adjustment.

Try both these approaches with your horse.
What happened? What did you learn?

An Independent Seat
I think that it is important for a rider to be able to maintain her own balance, and that of the horse, independent of the reins. If you can't do that you don't have an independent seat, irrespective of how many years you may have ridden!

In a safe, enclosed space, such as an indoor school, ensure a large loop on long reins and try walk, trot and canter and simple transitions. How did you get on?

If it is safe to do so, tie a knot in your reins and drop them completely. Try the transitions and changes of rein. How did you get on?

I tried this experiment with an acquaintance. She couldn't trust herself to do it. I literally had to go over and pull the reins through her hands. Then she couldn't influence her horse at all. In her view this meant that "it didn't work" (not only was there no immediate improvement, things actually got a lot worse). She decided that I was wrong.

What do you think?

When I was first learning about contact it always felt fragile. I'd hold my breath because I didn't want to disturb it. Then, of course, I lost it. I'd have it on the circle and then my trainer would say "go large". There would be a rush of anxiety (could I keep it or not). I'd hope and pray I would succeed, then become very fixed and lose it.

What advice would you have given me?

In the 90's I attended a lecture-demonstration by Anky van Grunsven at Addington Equestrian Centre. Her words still ring in my ears. "Give rein, GIVE rein". At one point she told the audience that she always feels like there is a little loop in the rein. I think that I understand now what Anky was saying, but for me it is not just the rein we need to give. To give the rein we have to "give" the whole body. You can't afford to be precious about it. You know when it will be ok because you have the connection in your seat, independent of, and therefore not dependent on, your hand.

It takes a long time to develop a sensitive seat. Riders often use the term "strong seat" or describe a process of "working on their position". This seems like the wrong choice of words to me. What we want is a sensitive influential seat that connects to the brain directly and is able to release, hold in different muscles for fractions of a second, feel weight distribution and so on.

Seat

What is the seat? Not a trick question as it has been the subject of a lot of controversy between trainers. My definition would be those parts of the body in contact with the horse that are weight-bearing. This means that the seat will include your thighs as well as your "bottom".

The best way to understand how much weight is carried on the thighs is to sit on your horse bareback. Many un-knowledgeable people will tell you that riding bareback is "cruel" to the horse as all your weight is concentrated into your seat bones which then create huge pressure on the horse's sensitive back structures. Those of us who have done it (and I, for one, rode bareback for many years on my Arab) will tell you that the weight is spread over a broad area with a lot on the thighs.

The concept of the "perfect seat"

This is talked about in many books but how often is it seen? More to the point how often do you feel you are perfect? What does it feel like? People talk about "long" legs; about feeling like a frog; about becoming a clothes peg; feeling as light as a feather. I have felt at times all of these feelings.

I have found the following "seat" recipe works well for me.
In walk – sit centrally in the saddle and allow your weight to sink down into your legs (long legged feeling). Don't push your weight down; take the leg away from the horse and feel even weight on seat bones, bring the legs back into light contact and release your weight into your seat. Do not collapse. The feeling is more of letting go. Then grow tall through your back by trying to put a gap between each vertebra (without losing weight in the seat) and soften your neck and jaw ...then repeat...let go and up. It is a constant process of assessing areas of tension in our body and releasing them. The Alexander Technique is a great help with this (covered in more detail in chapter 8).

We have to be patient with ourselves and wait for it to happen...not trying to make it happen. In this way you use your skeleton to effectively support your weight so that your muscles are free to be released and free of tension. Release your hips to follow the movement – feel the hind legs coming under – left, right, left, right. As the right hind comes under, the right seat bone is carried forwards and down. This is learning to avoid any influence. We are in "listening" mode. Understanding "what is"; the freedom of the steps; the strength of the steps; his willingness to go forwards; his straightness. This is what some call a passive seat.

A good seat is a balanced seat. This means that ideally 50% of your weight is in the left half of your body and 50% in your right half. I say ideally because there is an intrinsic problem. We humans are all one sided and prefer to use one side of our body more than the other. Muscle is heavier than fat so the better muscled side will be heavier. To improve our riding we need to work on becoming more even. You can make a start now. If you are right-handed consciously inhibit holding this book in your right hand and hold it in your left. For a longer term intervention, try Pilates (see chapter 8 for more details).

Let your weight into your legs and feet – not pushing but letting go – feeling the support of the saddle and the horse's back and letting him carry you...going with the flow of energy......letting it be. Find the way into the movement by releasing and feeling, not by "doing". And certainly not by actively pushing with the seat. This only makes it more difficult for the horse to move forwards and gives you sore seat-bones. Believe me, I tried it!

Physics tells us that objects with lower centres of gravity are more stable. Generally speaking, wider and shorter makes for more stability; shapes with weight distributed lower down are more stable. This is why double pony trailers tend to be better balanced than single horse ones. The chassis on the trailer also adds to the comfort of the ride. This needs to be stable but not rigid otherwise the horses would bounce around with every slight change in road surface. The "chassis" for our seat is our pelvis and the muscles around it – our "core" muscles!

The same principle applies when we ride. We need to allow our centre of gravity to be as low as possible. A broader, squatter shape is better than a taller narrower one. How can we achieve this? Let the weight down into your lower body and thighs (remember, seat = knee to waist). Breathe in to the back of your ribs; as you breathe out let all your insides sink down whilst maintaining the structure of your bones (ie don't collapse your spine). Check that your ribs haven't flared out and they have release them down again. Release in the area where your leg joins on; then stabilise the upper body above this and let the lower leg hang. Feel the support of the stirrups on the ball of your foot. Don't push your heel down as some trainers might tell you. Just feel the support of the stirrup and let your weight sink down into your heel. Think it down. But do nothing active!

This is not something we do once when we ride. We do it ALL THE TIME. It is a full time job.

Keep an image of a big-bottomed rider in your mind and think how it would feel to be him. Make your rise smaller in rising trot. Feel that your seat is so heavy that you can hardly move out of the saddle in your rise.

Figure 21 Forces on the rider's body

The shock absorber in the lower back is very important. Think of the small of your back as a thick spring. If we make ourselves too tall we pull the spring and when held there we have no springiness (elasticity). If we collapse our weight down and draw our legs up the spring is totally compressed – again no springiness! The spring can only work well when it is at its natural length and aligned (not bent). This is what body-workers call "pelvic neutral".

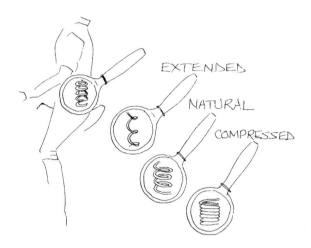

Figure 22 The Spring in the Back

Pelvic neutral allows us to go passively with the horse's movement. It lets the horse's energy pass through us without blockage or pushing. As our riding skills improve we can use our pelvis as we would the clutch in a car. Rotating our pelvis back pushes our seatbones forwards and this has a reinforcing (pushing) effect on the horse. Rotating our pelvis forwards pushes our seatbones backwards and this has a holding effect on the horse. It makes it more difficult for him to work through us. We must be careful to keep the energy and never block with the hand when using our pelvis in this way. We can experiment with small changes to our pelvis angle to really understand the power of this tool.

Watch good riders riding. What do you see? Where are they absorbing all that movement? Different riders absorb it in different places. Really good riders absorb it inside. If it is not absorbed inside it will be visible outside. If the seat stays connected but the overall movement is not absorbed then this is when we tend to see nodding heads and wobbly shoulders.

Where do you absorb the movement?

Legs

We have to somehow or other get our leg underneath us so that we can carry our selves. Our position is neither sitting nor standing, it is in-between. It is more like squatting. Many people find it difficult to squat in balance on the ground – never mind on a moving animal! This is our challenge!

Mary Wanless is very specific about recommended leg angles in her book "Ride with your mind essentials" (9): 100 degrees for experienced riders and 90 degrees for novices. Her words stimulated me to trawl through books and magazines and measure the angles of riders I admired. I discovered a wider angle between thigh and calf in pictures I admired than Mary recommends, commonly around 110-120 degrees.

William Micklem has different advice in his book "The Complete Horse Riding Manual" (5). For dressage he recommends 120-130 degrees. For jumping 105-115 degrees (but if you are short and the horse is big, it may help to ride a little longer). William says, "the wider a horse is, the shorter the stirrups must be. This is because as the distance between the knees increases, the knee and hip joint have to close to allow the lower leg to be in a vertical line and stay in contact with the horse's sides."

I find the shape of the horse's back and the impact on the rider to be very interesting. On a flatter backed horse the rider will naturally carry more weight on her thighs and this will naturally spread the load for the horse over a broader area. On a more slender creature it is even more vital to get the heel under the rider's centre of gravity as more weight will naturally flow down in to the foot. If this does not happen then the slender horse feels more weight in the riders seat – on the most sensitive section of his back! Ouch! I have noticed that slender horses tend to be more sensitive than their wider counterparts. Perhaps this is part of the reason why? And also why beginners are better on cobs? A more experienced rider can achieve more with the slender sensitive horse as her ability to hold her weight off her thighs gives more aid alternatives.

Look at classical engravings such as those in Paul Belasik's book – Dressage for the 21st Century" (7). The classical baroque riders are portrayed with legs almost straight ie nearly 180 degrees! Is this an honest representation of what the artist actually saw? Is it even physically possible? Is it a good thing for the horse? I think that many dressage riders think "I do dressage now so I lengthen my stirrups". What matters most in dressage is balance not stirrup length. We should set our stirrups to a length where we feel we are balanced. Longer is not necessarily better!

> *Is this all there is to it? What do you think? What affects leg position?*

Here are some factors I think have an effect on leg position:
- Length of rider's thigh and calf bones
- Shape of horse's barrel – depth, curvature
- Type of saddle eg GP, dressage, jumping
- Depth of seat on saddle
- Size and positioning of knee and/or thigh rolls
- Type of riding eg jumping, flatwork, hunting, dressage
- Fit of saddle to horse
- Fit of saddle to rider
- Position of stirrup bars
- Position and stability of rider's upper body

Breathing is a great help! You can learn to breathe in such a way that you assist your riding. Pilates and swimming have taught me the power of coordinating my breathing with my movement. My breathing can make me stronger and/or more relaxed. Breathe out as you sit – as you ask for any change. Many of us fail to use our breathing effectively and yet it is an amazing tool. Breathing helps us connect our mind to our body. Most of us take very shallow breaths and, as a result, fail to work the muscles in our chest. Try breathing in through your nose and out through your mouth. Try sucking in air through your nose using your throat. We can breathe in to different parts of our body. Breathing out emphasises letting go and relaxation.

We can develop our balanced seat best by
-   Being lunged. The Spanish Riding School advocates this method. But some of us don't have the luxury of another person to help us in this way.
-   "Lunging your-self". There is no third party involved here. The point is that you are riding purely with the intention of working on yourself. This is explained in more detail in the section on Initial Assessment and warm up in chapter 9.

Remember that in riding, as in life, we become strong by letting go not by hanging on.

Many books and riding instructors focus on what I call the externals of the rider's position. I don't think that this helps at all. It just makes us more and more fixed and less and less acceptable to our horse. Indeed, trying to mimic the position of another rider will never work.

Instead of focusing on straight lines here and there go inside yourself and focus on feel. You need to be
-   Balanced
-   Relaxed
-   "With" the movement (harmonious not blocking).
When you are all of these things then your position as it appears on the outside will be perfect for you and your horse!

An open focus – internal or external
A major problem area for me has been my focus. I often find myself focussing on an area just in front of saddle and my horse's head and ears. This undoubtedly tips me forward. It makes it more difficult for my horse in transitions as I am loading his forehand.

Stand without shoes with your feet directly beneath your hips. Look at a point at eye height ahead and rise up onto your toes. Now tip your head forward. What happens? When we ride we must ensure we are looking forwards at eye height.

Be proud; no apologies, aware of everything but not focusing on any one thing. To do this we need to relax our eyes. Release tension in your eyes by thinking of breathing out through them. Sally Swift describes this as "soft eyes" in her book Centred Riding (12).

In riding, our eyes affect our ability to feel as well as to see. When we stop seeing our feeling sense is heightened. Whilst mounted try closing your eyes and feeling the weight in the rein. Whilst dismounted try focussing your eyes on something at eye height and standing on one leg. Now close your eyes. *What happens?*

For good riding we need to strike a better balance between seeing and feeling (internally or externally focussed). We see but it is not our main focus. Our main focus is feeling inside. Most of us are probably 90% external and 10% internal. We need to rebalance not just for riding but for life!

Testing the quality of the connection
We can test the quality of our connection by giving away one or both of the reins.

What could happen when we give away the rein? What does it mean?

The horse falls onto his forehand and rushes? Why? The horse was relying on the hand for support...and/or the horse is not sufficiently connected to the riders seat. Why? Maybe the horse is not strong enough to complete the movement or has lost balance for some other reason or is fatigued.

The horse hollows? Why? The head was being "held down" by the rider. Perhaps the horse has been trained in draw reins. Why?

The horse comes into a beautiful poll high, nose in front of the vertical carriage? Why? The horse was held in front by a rider who already has the horse in her seat. I have seen this with some very capable riders.

The horse opens the angle under the jaw? Why? As previously, but perhaps the horse is more novice. I have witnessed this when I allowed a strong rider to ride my young novice horse.

The last two results are likely to happen when the horse is over-bent as a result of a rider with too strong a hand. Note that a horse that was over-bent because it was avoiding the bit (ie behind the bit) will likely stay the same when the rein is given!

The desirable result is that the horse gently lengthens his frame to seek the same contact at a point further forward. The rider encourages and supports this stretching and relaxation with her seat.

Giving the rein is a brilliant exercise and should be done frequently to test self carriage or to enable stretching and relaxation of muscles. To test self carriage give either one or both reins. Is the same frame and rhythm and balance maintained?

To encourage stretching allow the rein to *gradually* get longer (often described as the horse chewing the rein out of the riders hand). If the rider just throws the rein at the horse she will really unbalance him. If he was in good carriage before he will feel a lot more weight in the bit from the given rein. This can be done in all 3 paces but with rhythm and balance maintained.

Never allow the horse to get his head too low and drop through his wither. This will push him onto his forehand and the horse will deposit the weight of his head in your hand or curl up and hang behind the vertical. Encourage the horse to stretch only to the point where he can maintain his balance. Be sure not to tip forwards yourself! If you do you will overburden his forehand. Instead, open the angle at the elbow and allow the reins to gradually get longer.

A good rider can achieve both these feels at will. She can give the rein and encourage stretching or seeking and can give the rein and retain the carriage in her seat.

At lower levels of dressage competitions the give and retake is asked for in canter and is often poorly executed. The free walk is asked for from Preliminary level and also provides a good test of the connection.

Sit in or write for a dressage judge in tests requiring a "give and retake". What is the variation in marks? What sort of comments did the judge make? How could the g&r's you saw be improved?

Things to remember
A good rein contact is light and consistent. It is achieved when we have "rein equilibrium".
Only when we can control ourselves can we have a good pair of hands. Only then the horse will seek a "rein equilibrium".
Successful stretching and give and retake exercises depend on the mechanics of "rein equilibrium".
A skilled rider can change the outline and maintain "rein equilibrium".
To improve our hands we must improve our balance which means that we must improve our seat.
The connection is proven by our ability to give it away.

6 Communication

We have our connection with the horse. Now we need to communicate with him to achieve our goals. Not only is communication enabled by the connection but also the right communication can strengthen the connections.

I like to think of a mindset for riding well. There are four parts to this mindset:

    (1)   Stop thinking about where I should be and focus on where I am now. Take an experimental approach to riding. "I wonder what happens if……" rather than "I must make it like this";

    (2)   "C'est pas grave" or in English "it doesn't matter". When things go wrong don't react or blame (yourself or the horse). Just try it again;

    (3)   Learning from mistakes. Diagnosing what went wrong and why. Trying something different;

    (4)   No sudden changes. To learn about a system we must test its sensitivity little by little – otherwise we create chaos.

Balance

The main topic of our conversation with the horse is BALANCE. Together the horse and I have to work out a language through which we can understand each other. I think that the process is very much trial and error or should I say trial, error, learning, trial...

To begin with we communicate to build mutual understanding and balance. We can then ask questions to test understanding and ability to maintain balance.

Have you ever tried to learn a new language? I am going through the process of learning French right now. I think that all riders should attempt to learn another human language themselves. That way they can understand better the process the horse is going through. I learn better with repetition; in context (ie it is useful); when I am closer (face to face is best); when it is "real" and there is a reason; when I feel I can have a go and be corrected without ridicule.

Because I don't think in French I have to stop and think how to say what I want to say in French. Sometimes I can't because I don't have the words. Then I have to think of other ways of saying the same thing. It is amazing. Often there are hundreds of slightly different ways of saying the same thing. This means that I must choose. Because I don't have to do this in English I don't really make a conscious choice. Sometimes I think it would be better to do this in English too… there is always another way.

The point I am trying to make is that it is good to think about communication before you do it. What impact are you trying to make? How could that be achieved? What is the best way to achieve it? It works for people. It works for horses. Don't give away the power to choose.

Stephen Covey (2), a renowned management consultant, states in his book, "The Seven Habits of Highly Effective People", that to do this we must first seek to understand then seek to be understood. But first of all, before seeking to understand others, I think we need to really understand ourselves…

Before we start a conversation or ask any question of our horse we must first ensure we are prepared by "questioning" ourselves. The full time job of the rider is balancing herself. Only by balancing herself can she minimise the burden to her horse. This involves becoming highly body aware.

The rider constantly assesses her balance and rebalances herself. Ensuring she is straight (even weight 50/50 Left to Right) and using only the minimum amount of tension in the muscles and releasing any excess tension. It is only possible to do this when our body comes into natural alignment. Then and only then can we "let go" and release our insides to where they would naturally like to be. This carriage and freedom allows the horse's energy to pass "through" us without any blocks. How can he move loose and free when we are stiff and blocking? The rider takes her attention inside herself; identifying areas of tension and releasing (literally thinking it free). Learning how to do this is the focus of the Alexander Technique (see chapter 8).

The rider does this before every change of direction, every transition and many times per minute. The external observer is unable to see this. The activity is internal and flowing. There is a lot going on but it is happening on the inside not the outside.

So, the rider feels and rebalances herself. Then she feels the horse and rebalances him using movements. On and on and on.........

No riding instructor taught me this. I learnt it myself from Alexander lessons and then experimented with it on the horse. The single thing that I do all the time when I'm riding and lunging well is something no-one told me!

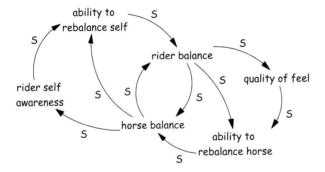

Figure 23 Balancing Loop "Balance"

I think that Sally Swift is referring to this in her "Centred Riding 2" (12) when she talks about "dropping a ball" down through herself. The rider half halts herself. And this half halts the horse. This doesn't involve the use of hands or legs. It is far more subtle.

Degrees of balance

A person is balanced in body when there is equal weight left and right. It is the same for our horse. Our balance is challenged when we try to do more difficult activities. For example, my balance could be fine to sit in a chair but can I walk a tightrope? Our horse is fine grazing in the field but what about galloping flat out down a muddy slope? Horse and rider can individually be balanced when static but movement will challenge that balance.

As a rider we need to constantly assess, reassess and re-balance – ie adjust weight distribution. To assess we need to find a "place" where we can feel – not just in our hand but in our whole body – a quiet place where we are literally doing nothing, where we become aware of our balance.

Many riders, myself included, suffer from an inability to "assess what is happening now", because we are too busy doing too much with our bodies and wanting to be somewhere else in our minds (by now I should be doing x,y,z with my horse). In this we miss out on understanding what we have NOW!

The horse can't find his balance if we are constantly changing things, niggling and interfering. The horse uses his head and neck to balance himself so you must interfere as little as possible with the horse's ability to do that. Cultivate a giving forwards hand that never blocks, not even momentarily. Trust that the horse will come into a beautiful carriage when he can. This may be after 5 minutes or 5 years! But it will come.

If you try to fake it by artificially positioning the horse's head with special equipment what will happen when you take away the support of this artificial aid? What do you want – look or feel? When it feels right it will look right – but it doesn't necessarily work the other way around. Think of riding the horse's ears forward away from you – think that you can make his neck longer. Never think of shortening his neck or "pulling him together" or fiddling his head down.

The horse can't "forgive" our bad riding because it affects his balance. But he will never bear malice and hold it against you in the next session! However, he does have a long memory and bad experiences are not easily forgotten. The horse lives in the moment and reacts to what is happening now. He doesn't think "oh last time she rode me she completely restricted my canter because of her seat so this time I'll show her and make it uncomfortable for her". He seems to know when we are trying to improve and is eternally patient with us. He is less patient when we are intentionally seeking to manipulate him.

Horses tend to do what we enable them to do. Unfortunately this is not always what we want! This means that we have to learn how to ask properly and not get in the way (and so make it as easy as possible for the horse to comply).

The true test of balance is when the horse carries himself and the rider, unaided, without support from the hand. This can be proven by giving away one or both reins or by riding with a loop in the reins with no change in the beautiful outline. It can also be tested by the horse seeking the rein forwards and down in walk on a long rein or similarly with trot and canter. I think that these movements should be given at least twice the marks in all dressage tests.

What factors affect balance?

Here are some ideas to get you started:
- Horse conformation, fitness and strength
- The shape of the rider and the horse
- Rider's "talent"
- Rider conformation and fitness
- Rider's ability to manage posture – body control
- Rider's ability to release tension – body awareness
- Base of support - connection to the ground
- Engagement of horse's hind legs
- Consistency of surface
- Confidence that you won't fall
- Gradient
- Balance challenge in movements

-   Consistency – an uneven load can be accommodated as long as it is consistently uneven.

What are the signs that you and/or your horse have lost balance?
This can manifest in a number of ways: lack of straightness, falling in/out on circles, rhythm changes, tempo changes, horse comes against hand/leans on hand, trips/falls over/stumbles.

What causes loss of balance?
The responsibility could be with the horse or the rider or a little of both. It doesn't really matter who is "to blame". What matters is recognising and correcting without overcorrecting. We have to pay attention to and manage balance every moment that we ride.

For example, in canter, if the rider tenses because she loses physical balance or tenses because she loses mental balance (eg oh no here comes that sticky corner again) she will unbalance the horse. In addition, the horse may himself become unbalanced. This may happen quickly through a change in the quality of the surface or a sudden change of direction. He may become unbalanced gradually, in canter becoming longer and longer and more and more on the forehand. Inevitably he will fall out of canter into a long and disorganised trot.

How do we recover balance?

The answer depends on the cause and how great the loss of balance actually is. Prevention is always better than cure. Usually prevention is through preparation.

Useful rebalancing exercises include –
-   Reducing speed (slowing the rhythm) – using the body, or if absolutely necessary, with the hand, but then giving to allow the horse to re-find his balance
-   Controlling the tempo with a controlling seat
-   The half halt
-   Reducing the pace – it is easier for the horse to balance himself in walk than trot, in halt than walk and so on

- Using the circle (remember a circle gives the opportunity for "no change")
- Using the school walls
- Using poles
- Not overdoing things - only do as much as balance can be maintained then reduce pace and start again. For example, it is better to have 6 good canter strides then transition to trot and repeat. In this way the rider gradually builds confidence by being able to reward him rather than waiting for him to fail! An excellent example of using this to teach the horse to counter canter is given in Michel Henriquet's book (10). He advocates riding a diagonal and then letting the horse make as many strides as possible and gradually building this up. The rider's task is to be a neutral force and allow the horse to work out how to keep his balance for himself.

Self carriage is a very interesting term, as it means more than balance to me. Carrying the self, taking responsibility for our own weight, is not just about our body-weight. The self is also the mind, so we must also take responsibility for the "weight of our mind", make good choices – fairly, and take responsibility for the outcomes. Yes, self carriage is as important in life as in riding..........

Attention – active listening
On a recent visit to the UK I met up with a horsey friend who I hadn't seen for some time. My non-horsey partner was with me at the time. My friend and I talked and talked and talked – you know how it is – I completely forgot about time and other visits we had promised to make to other folk.

Afterwards my partner told me that he had been getting more and more frustrated with me. He told me I had been ignoring his signs to leave on purpose. I told him that I hadn't even noticed him making any signs. That was the truth!

What should my partner have done?
What does it teach us about interacting with our horse?

I think the moral of the story is that to communicate we need attention. To receive this attention we must be more compelling than the distractions. With the highest levels of attention and trust we have the ability to stay focussed despite the chaos around us. This is probably best witnessed in the dressage competition world...those with attention and trust are better able to perform in the most trying circumstances.

We can keep attention by frequent change of direction, of pace, of exercise. We must strike a balance between change to maintain attention and avoid boredom and repetition to reinforce learning.

Communication - Correction and Reward
Having a constant conversation with our horse helps maintain attention. This conversation consists of listening, questioning, repeating, explaining, encouraging, reassuring and praising.

We start by listening. On horseback this means understanding how our horse is feeling in his body and his mind. Is he energetic or lazy? Is he stiff or free? Where is he stiff? Do I have his attention or is he spooky? And so on. This enables us to craft questions that help to further diagnose issues, or help to address the issue.

What questions do we ask?
When do we ask?
How do we ask?
How do we respond to his behaviour?

We work on the enablers within our influence – more or less energy, degree of bend, engagement, cadence, length of stride, outline (length of frame), direction (forwards/ backwards/ sideways), degree of difficulty (ie challenge to balance) of movements.

If he is stiff we need to understand why he is stiff. Maybe he has just come out of the stable and needs more time to warm up. Maybe we could have warmed him up more before by turning him out or putting him on a walker or lunging or massage or all of these! If we are sure we have done all we can in this way then we must devise ridden exercises to stretch those stiff muscle groups.

Experiment. *Did it help? Why not? What have I learnt? What could I try next?*

When to ask?
Timing is of the essence in communicating with our horse. The sequence of each pace and the quality of that pace will dictate the quality of the transition. There are good and bad times to ask for transitions. Good timing increases our likelihood of success. Poor transitions are often the result of bad timing! We riders must understand how the horse moves in each pace, to feel and know when the time is right. For example, the horse strikes off into canter with the outside hind leg. It makes sense, therefore, to ask for the upwards transition as the outside hind is about to leave the ground. To do this we have to feel the sequence of leg movements through our seat. We can also exploit our external circumstances, for example asking for canter as we enter a corner.

How do we ask?
It is not the purpose of this book to talk about aids as they are well covered in other literature, save one point. In French "Aider" means "to help" – so aids are not instructions, they are "helps" – ways of helping or enabling (allowing) our horse. Think - how can I help my horse to understand? What are the choices? What are the likely consequences of each choice? Make your choice and be definite. Follow through to understand whether it worked and if not why not. On and on and on... never ending.

So how can we help our horse to understand us?

I think that the honest answer can be however we want. We can train our horses to our voice, to the clicker, to the leg, to the seat. Whatever we choose. Some of these will be acceptable in competition, others will not. You can have your own private communication system with your horse. It can be that personal.

> *How does this make you feel? Do you feel excited or threatened at this point?*

Inger Bryant (List 1 Dressage Judge) agreed with me on this but said that horses, like humans, can learn multiple languages (communication systems). She works a lot with disabled riders who are unable to aid the horse in conventional terms. She argues that we owe it to our horses' future to always teach the common language of aids. In this way our horse can be of use to others and so always has the possibility of a new life with others.

William Micklem (5) in his book, "The Complete Horse Riding Manual" also states that " The difference in aid systems used by different trainers can create problems. A horse that learns to canter from an aid with the outside leg will not understand a canter aid from the inside leg, while a rider's effectiveness will be reduced if they have to keep changing aids."

I can see the points Inger and William are making but don't really understand how this can be achieved. A rider riding a horse for the first time will have to find what degree of aiding is necessary. To the horse each rider will feel different as we are all different shapes and sizes. Personally I don't believe that there can be a universal language for the horse as we don't even have a universal language for humans. Not only do we have different base languages, eg English, French etc, we also have different accents and local dialects!

The horse's response?
The horse can respond in different ways.

The horse says "YES" by doing what we have asked, effortlessly. Brilliant! We reward him by telling him he' s good, and by not repeating the question.

If he says "NO" by not doing it or by doing it badly then we must think about why. Does he understand what we want? If not have patience – this is learning. See how you can help him out and repeat the exercise.

If he does understand check yourself. Ask yourself, is it me? If it is, then correct yourself. If not then it is time to be firmer.

When his efforts please us we reward our horse, reinforcing his positive behaviour, and encouraging him to try harder when we next ask. When the result is less pleasing we must think – what happened and why did it happen? The result of this analysis will enable us to choose the best correction. Often the correction is in ourselves. We monitor the result and then choose to reward, correct or move on to ask another question...and so the conversation continues.

How big a correction should I make?
The answer is to be as soft as you can be and as hard as you need to be.

Sometimes you find yourself lacking in knowledge of options for correction. Better to take time out and research alternative ways forward and implications.

Generally, I think that if there is no physical reason that the horse cannot do as you are asking it is better to make a large and deliberate correction and then give. Ignoring the problem does not make it go away.

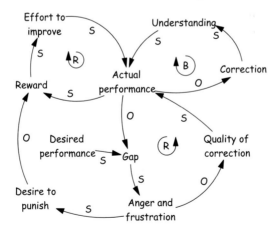

Figure 24 Feedback: Correction and Reward

This process is described in a CLD in figure 24. The better the quality of the performance, the more we reward our horse, the more he tries harder for us and the better the performance. A reinforcing loop. The poorer the quality of the performance, the more we correct our horse, the better he understands what we are asking for and the better the performance.

This requires self control. All too often we are dissatisfied with the gap between what we have and what we aspire to. This can create frustration and anger which can detract from the quality of our correction and create a desire to punish rather than to reward. It is for this reason that the old masters tell us that we must be delighted with small improvements.

For the horse to do what we want he must understand what we want him to do. He must be able to do it. And he must want to do it.
The "understanding" is all about the quality of his previous training and the quality of our current communication.

The "ability to do" is generally physical in nature. Are we unintentionally blocking the movement we have asked for. Is our horse too fatigued?

"Wanting to do" is mental. We can reinforce the horse's own natural motivation by using reward and anticipation. Like people, though, there are some horses that just can't be bothered. These horses are best left to riders wanting a challenge!

For each failure in communication we must try to understand why. Only then can we make the most appropriate correction.

Let me illustrate these points with some examples.
Example 1
Eric, my Lusitano, runs through my hand into halt.
Why? Maybe he isn't listening. Maybe he can't do it.
Give him the benefit of the doubt, check myself and my preparation, and ask nicely again. Still ignoring me.

Why? He just seems to want to keep going. He is in a world of his own! What should I do next?

Trying the same thing again with no reaction will only enforce his understanding that he can ignore things. So, either I do something else to get his attention eg a small circle before halting, or I use my hand as I ask for halt in the same place, and give immediately.

I reluctantly decide to make a point and use my hand. He is surprised, but halts promptly. I pat him to reassure him he has done the right thing. I repeat the exercise in the same place. He halts immediately. Much praise and do something else.

Example 2
Eric falls out of canter.
Why? He lost his balance!
Why did he lose his balance? I lost my balance and blocked him with my hand! Why did I lose my balance? My weight went too much to the outside on the corner.
Why did that happen? I wasn't paying attention.
Why? I was bored.
What should I do next? Focus my attention, rebalance myself and ask for the canter again. Reward as soon as I can. Then move onto something else I find less boring.

Example 3
Eric falls out of canter.
Why? He lost his balance!
Why did he lose his balance? He was tired.
Why was he tired? I'd asked for too much without a recovery period.
What should I do next? Regain his attention, rebalance him and ask for the canter again. After a few good strides, back to trot and praise him. Then down to walk. Give him a long rein and leave it there for the day. Make a mental note not to overdo it next time and to be more aware of early signs of fatigue.

Example 4
Eric falls out of canter.
Why? He lost his balance!
Why did he lose his balance? He lost concentration when the cat moved in the corner of the school.
Why? He wasn't listening to me.
What should I do next? Regain his attention, rebalance him and ask for the canter again. Reward as soon as I can.

Example 5
Eric falls out of canter.
Why? Because I'm a poor rider!
Whilst this may be the case it doesn't help with our problem does it? A better response would be as for example 1. Try to be specific about what happened – only then can we work on improvement.

So we
1.   Prepare by balancing ourselves;
2.   Ask the right question;
3.   Assess (Feel);
4.   Reward and return to 1; or
5.   Analyse and Correct and return to 2.

Podhajsky in his "Complete Training" (14) uses the terms punishment (as opposed to correction) and reward. For me punishment is a very strong word and should only be reserved for naughtiness rather than lack of effort or inadequate attempts. Punishment and learning do not sit very well together.

I recently visited a yard in the UK. A beautiful young horse was being lunged in the indoor school. Silence except for the rhythmic sheath noise. Many piles of droppings litter the school surface. Round and round in trot and canter. The purpose of the work was to take away the excess energy before he was mounted for the first time.

Each time the trainer approached the horse to change the rein he "attacked" her with his teeth or his front legs. I was shocked. At this point the owner of the yard, and the horse, walked over with a lunge whip and hit the horse. I was shocked. She returned to me and said the horse was a problem and that the only person that could control him was her husband, who hit him with a pipe!

At no point did I see this horse get a reward – only correction or should I say punishment. What I saw was fear. The humans feared the horse and the horse feared them. Each was unable to trust the other.

> *What would you have done if you were me?*
> *Now imagine the owner asked you for advice. What would it be?*

Tension

Muscular tension in the rider can be caused by either mental or physical problems. Low confidence leaves us fearful and tense (literally clinging on with our muscles). The feeling in our mind involuntarily affects our body and leads to hard muscles. In turn this means that the horse is blocked by the rider and is tense also. Muscle tension can also result from injury. The body tenses involuntarily to protect itself. Once again the horse is blocked by the rider and is tense also.

High levels of confidence can bring similar problems. Such self belief can lead to domination ("he will do this") and force. This can lead to voluntarily tensed and hard muscles. In turn this means that the horse is blocked by the rider. At times I have indulged in this behaviour. "I must make him do this…by now I should be doing this"…but fail to recognise what I or the horse feel like today and that it isn't going to be possible. This is a recipe for frustration and anger. I'm sure we have all been there.

> *Can you think of times when you have been too demanding? What happened? Why? What did you learn?*

Persistence

When to persist and when to desist? Some coaches believe that persistence is all important. I disagree. I think that the skill is knowing when to persist and when to desist. And this means understanding the system! In that way we don't walk away when one more try would fix it, and equally we don't persist in the face of inevitable failure. Persistence which results in self destruction is defeating.

Definiteness

Definiteness is not about being apologetic. It is not about being forceful. It is about being clear and consistent. The problem often seen is that the rider does not feel confident enough to correct the horse when she herself feels she may be the cause of the problem. Eyes on the ground can help to check that you are sitting straight and so on. Often it is just that the lack of confidence results in a lack of definiteness and the horse just thinks it's ok. The rider knows it isn't and blames themself again.

"If only I was good enough everything would be ok" – oh I know that statement so well! The truth that practice makes permanent can bring fear to those lacking in self belief. The conclusion may be that it is better not to practice at all…

The greater the rider's confidence, the more she acts positively. This means our horse is clearer about what we want and inspires him to trust us. Clarity of communication and confidence increases the willingness of our horse to work for us and this in turn improves the confidence of the rider. A powerful reinforcing loop. Wallowing in self-blame and pity changes nothing. Recognise that, and you're on your way forward.

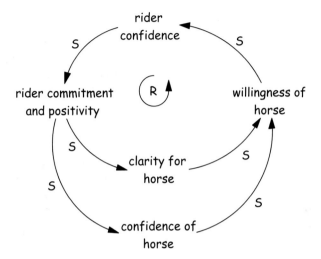

Figure 25 Vicious spiral of definiteness

Know you know

Once you know – remember that you know! If you revisit things you already know in the processing side of your brain you waste valuable processor time and become confused and limit yourself. Self belief is a tremendously powerful force.

One trainer used to say to me "I wish you'd ride like you drive". At the time I didn't really understand what he meant. Now I think that I do. I knew that I knew how to drive so I didn't think about how to do it; it just happened naturally. Unlike a beginner driver ...or indeed trying a new car (especially left hand drive!). The minute you start thinking about how to do it the flow stops. It becomes mechanical, jerky and not flowing.

Things to remember

The quality of our connection with our horse affects the quality of communication and vice versa.

Balance is the key topic of dialogue with our horse.

We must understand balance: the factors affecting it and how we can rebalance ourself and our horse.

To communicate we must have attention.

Listen; choose an exercise; assess impact (listen to horse's response)

Reward a little with much; correct much with little.

Successful communication depends on knowing when to ask and how to ask.

Anger is self defeating.

Be committed and definite.

Be honest with yourself and your horse.

7 The Dynamics of Training

In Chapter 2 we explored the objectives of riding. We quoted the FEI: "The object of dressage is the development of the horse into a happy athlete through harmonious education. As a result, it makes the horse calm, supple, loose and flexible, but also confident, attentive and keen, thus achieving perfect understanding with his rider."(1)

Inger Bryant (List 1 dressage judge) summarised her training objectives as "First I aim to have the horse **understand** what we want and second to develop his **physical ability**."

In chapter 3 we learnt about the mental models we hold in our heads. "The way we think the world works". We saw how Systems Thinking (ST) gives us a language for sharing and improving our mental models and a philosophy for making better choices. We saw that unless we trace and fix the root causes of our problems we will be unable to progress in a sustainable way.

In chapters 4 to 6 we applied ST to learn how, by strengthening our connection with our horse, we can improve our communication and so understand each other better. When we have this understanding we can use it to train ourselves and our horses.

In this chapter we will use ST to explore the cause and effect relationships at work in training. In this way, we can understand the potential choices we can make in our training. We explore what we need to work on to train our horses to perform sustainably and with lightness.

Correct musculature
Horses, like humans, are born with unbalanced musculature and a preference for a certain side. Typically one side will be more flexible and stretchy and the other stronger. Our horse's best rein will be the one where his powerful side is on the inside and his stretchy one on the outside. For efficiency and to prevent injuries we need to work towards making our horse's musculature more even.

Good muscles are of natural length. They are neither contracted (making them strong but inflexible) or overstretched (making them flexible but weak). This means that we must work on suppling our horse – stretching his strong contracted muscles to improve flexibility and strengthening his weaker ones to make them more powerful. Both flexibility and strength are necessary to perform well and sustainably. Weakness and inflexibility leave our horse vulnerable to injury.

If we demand that our horse perform exercises that are above his capability given his musculature he will incur injuries and unsoundness which in turn will lead to loss of muscle due to lack of work. This means that we must work on the boundaries of our horse's capability. We must ensure that new exercises are introduced when he has sufficient energy and are devised in such a way to help build the necessary muscles as he learns. It goes without saying that it will be more difficult to develop muscle correctly on a poor or crooked frame. Conformation has a great impact on what will be possible. On the other hand, weaker conformation can be supported with correct muscles.

A good example of this is my old horse, Shantie. Amongst his many problems are a club foot and one front leg longer than the other. Luckily for him no-one ever told him this and he was very successful in local show jumping competitions.

Working with imbalanced musculature will always involve a degree of tension. This makes movement difficult and so it involves more effort than is necessary. It looks laboured and it is. It will become easier when he has developed the correct musculature and he uses that musculature with minimum effort. When this happens our horse moves with ease and feels like he could carry on the work forever (like freewheeling on a bike).

The most efficient shape for any athlete is symmetrical – even left to right – and even top to bottom (head to tail). Most horses are naturally built to carry more weight on the forehand. The weight of a rider adds to this problem. To address this we have to develop our horse so that he is able to carry more weight behind. This allows him to carry a rider more easily and gives freedom to the shoulders so that all movement becomes lighter and easier. We call this a collected frame. It is the most efficient way of carrying and propelling the weight of horse and rider.

To achieve this redistribution of weight the rider "collects" the horse. In other words she helps him to work in a more mechanically efficient frame. This requires two things: impulsion and alignment (straightness – the hind feet following in the path of the fore feet). The first priority is straightness as energy without straightness does not give impulsion. It gives wasted energy!

To improve straightness we need to reduce muscle tension in the horse to the minimum necessary for the exercise in hand. The absence of unnecessary tension is often called relaxation or decontraction. The two are inter-related as the more the horse relaxes his tense muscles the more he will straighten, and the straighter he is the more he can release excess tension as his balance improves.

Our horse will not be able to release tension in his body if he is tense and anxious in his mind. The rider needs to cultivate calmness. Calmness is affected by many things; the sensitivity of the horse; the way he is managed (in the stable or field); the spookiness of the environment (eg wind, unfamiliar surroundings etc); his level of understanding and trust in his rider.

We can try to control our environment but this is not always possible. We can decide not to ride eg when it is windy. We can desensitise our horse by riding him in lots of different environments. We can build his confidence in us by being consistent and clear in our training and by managing our own calmness.

A key factor in developing calmness is rhythm. Rhythm has a calming effect on the horse's mind. It stimulates endorphin production which in turn allows him to feel and release unwanted tension in his body. This gives us an important feedback loop. Rhythm affects calmness which in turn affects relaxation which in turn improves the regularity of the rhythm. This loop is reinforcing in that whichever direction it starts with (virtuous or vicious) this will continue as long as nothing changes.

I think that it is difficult to work on rhythm directly without becoming too fixed and stiff ourselves. Rather, I think that we work on keeping ourselves calm and relaxed and keeping things "the same". As our horse calms his rhythm will improve. This means that we work on calmness and through this influence rhythm.

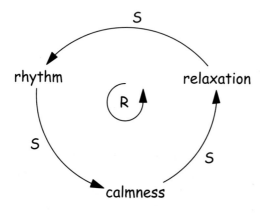

Figure 26 Developing rhythm

It is difficult to breathe deeply and evenly when we are tense. It is the same for our horse. Signs that our horse is calming include relaxed snorting. This shows he is letting go and is breathing more calmly. Contrast this with the forced angry snorting which is a sign of high anxiety. If we focus on our breathing and relaxation we will influence our calmness and in turn our horse's calmness.

An even rhythm is best achieved by "no change". The easiest place to achieve this is in trot on a true circle. Equally repetitive exercises of any kind can be soothing and calming. Lunging is also a great help for similar reasons. It allows the horse to develop rhythm and balance without the additional problem of the weight of the rider.

The best demonstration I have seen of this was watching John Micklem lunging my anxious Arab, Shantie. As I watched Shantie careering around and around in what I considered to be rather a dangerous fashion I asked John what he was doing about it. John said that he was doing nothing because there was nothing he could do. He was simply waiting for Shantie to calm down and relax. He explained that as this happened Shantie would find his own natural regular rhythm. And it was true. I watched it happen.

An unsound horse will have an irregular rhythm due to tension and compensation. A horse will lose rhythm whenever he loses his balance. This means that rhythm is a symptom of calmness. We pay attention to it but we only influence it through our own calmness.

An anxious horse who is tense in the mind will not be able to focus solely on his rider. He will not be attentive. We can work on attentiveness by working on calmness. We can also work on calmness by improving attentiveness. This is another important feedback loop. As a horse's trust in his rider increases so will his calmness. Trust requires consistency.

If our horse isn't listening to us and is not calm we need to get his attention through exercises that are calming and engage his brain. A good example would be lots of lateral work in walk. Fast work and transitions are less appropriate at this time.

If he is calm but inattentive (ie switched off) we can work on both with faster work and lots of transitions. Be clear and consistent. The more responsive he gets the more the encouragement to reinforce his confidence.

We could get our lazy horse's attention by cracking him with a whip. This is likely to be counter-productive as we create anxiety, lose calmness and increase muscle tension – not such a clever intervention after all!

As our horse's body de-contracts, his back softens and he becomes more comfortable to sit on. As a result he finds us easier to carry. Another reinforcing loop.

As the connection strengthens he becomes more attentive and, as a result, more responsive to our requests. He becomes more ride-able and open to our influence. We can use this to improve his alignment and make him more responsive.

As he becomes more responsive we can start to develop impulsion. We can ask for more energy and we can direct it more forwards through his straighter, decontracted frame.

Exercise uses oxygen from the air to power the muscles, converting the energy from food. It is sustainable for periods that depend upon the amount of effort the horse puts in. If the horse is working at very high exercise levels, he becomes tired. Without a proper recovery period between vigorous spells of exercise, the horse will feel pain in his muscles. This leads to tension and reduced ability to focus.

Balancing feed and exercise is very important. A fit horse is not a fat horse. Carrying fat on horse or rider means inefficiency and increased effort for any given outcome. This means that we have to ensure our horse has adequate fuel (food) for his work requirements and no more. We have to balance energy input through diet, and energy utilisation through living and working.

The Scales of Training
The British Dressage (41) Rules 2006 Appendix 10 states that "The most tried and tested ways of understanding the way of going are the German Scales of Training. These are what the riders in the most successful dressage nation in the world learn in their early years of riding and what the leading international judges talk about at the seminars they give.

Those Scales of Training are:
Rhythm
Suppleness
Contact
Impulsion
Straightness
And eventually, Collection.

Despite the investment in training around the scales I believe that there is still a lot of misunderstanding amongst riders, trainers and judges. One person who responded to my survey offered the following interpretation of the scales:

"...Rhythm must come before relaxation and relaxation before you can establish a correct contact and a correct contact before you can develop impulsion which needs suppleness and elasticity. When these are confirmed you can work on straightness and only then on collection."

Erik Herbermann reinforces this understanding in his book, The Dressage Formula (4) – "One must have each single requirement before the next step can be attained".

Can you identify the problem with this logic?

This statement describes riding as a linear progression. It fails to recognise that the concepts are variables and that there are many cause and effect relationships between these variables.

We like to break things down and simplify them but riding is not like that. Complexity is fact. If we fail to understand the complexity and the interrelationships we will fail to improve the performance of the system in a lasting way. We may see an improvement in the short term but in the end we will fail. Moreover, we will also fail to communicate and share our understanding in a meaningful way.

Inger Bryant (List 1 dressage judge) told me "first I aim to have the horse understand what we want and second to develop his physical ability". I believe this applies equally to riders as horses. But how many training establishments truly integrate theory and practice?

Capturing my client's business strategies in Systems Thinking (ST) diagrams was a key element of my previous career. It was never easy to do this as few strategies are expressed in the clear, unambiguous style required by ST. It is the same with riding books and other sources of instruction. And without direct access to each author it is difficult to confirm the true intention in all cases.

The official Handbook of the German National Equestrian Federation "The Principles of Riding" (6), does explain the cause and effect inter-relationships between the elements of the scale. Other books on training, notably those by Wolfgang Niggli (29)and Podhajsky (14) also explain their mental models in words. However, in all cases I find it very difficult to grasp "the whole" and there are many unresolved inconsistencies.

Here I will aim to share my understanding of the cause and effect relationships at work and how they affect the horse's way of going.

Collection

The rider is responsible for training her horse. Her goal is higher levels of collection. But what is this thing we are aiming for? What is collection? How do we know we are achieving it? Until we have understood it we have little chance of achieving it!

The Global Dressage Forum glossary of judging terms 2007 (28) states that "The horse shows collection when he lowers and engages his hindquarters – shortening and narrowing his base of support, resulting in lightness and mobility of the forehand."

How is this achieved?

Tension is the enemy of collection. This means that we must train our horse to use only the muscles required for the movement, with no excess tension. In this way we develop his core strength and his flexibility. We develop the muscles in his hind quarters to enable him to carry more weight behind which allows him to collect himself and so improves his balance. Higher levels of collection allow us to achieve self carriage which in turn means more lightness.

What is lightness? The term lightness is often used but ambiguous and therefore potentially misleading. Lightness can mean sensitivity or responsiveness. This is about the horse's reaction to our influence. It may imply that he reacts more quickly and/or to a smaller signal. I prefer to think of this form of lightness as responsiveness. Lightness can also refer to the weight the rider feels in the rein. We have already discussed this form of lightness in chapter 4. Lightness may also be used to describe the horse's way of going. The quality of the steps can be light, elastic, cadenced and soft; like a ballerina. They can also be heavy, dragging like an elephant. Balance and poise go hand in hand with this form of lightness.

Another school of thought assumes collection to mean "balance". The implication is that the horse has collection sufficient for a movement when there is no loss of balance. I have some sympathy with this view in that I can see loss of balance is one potential consequence of a lack of sufficient collection. But I don't believe that they are one and the same thing.

Others believe collection refers to the movement or pace. So, for example, a pirouette is a collected movement and collected trot is a collected pace.

Another point of view is that collection is about the lowering of the quarters achieved by the bending of the joints in the hind legs. It is about redistributing the burden of carrying weight. Theresa Sandin provides an excellent explanation of this aspect of collection on her website (16).

Naturally the horse carries more weight on his forehand. This makes his movement less mechanically efficient. So we train him to carry more of the weight behind. This lightens the forehand, enhances the freedom of the paces and places more weight under the "engine". To develop the strength necessary to do this takes many years of correct training. I think that what is being described here is the attainment of a very high level of collection.

Have you ever watched a horse approaching and preparing to jump a fence of decent height? To jump well the horse has to adjust himself to bring his weight back over his pushing hind legs at the point of take off. When allowed the freedom, the horse collects himself naturally in preparation for the task in hand. The same happens in a downwards transition. The horse will look to lift his head, neck and back as he does this. The rider must allow this to happen with her body.

I believe that posture and balance don't define collection. Rather they are symptoms of collection having been achieved. The term collection comes from the French verb "rassembler" which literally means to collect. But this begs a question. What is it that we are collecting?

Baucher, another eminent French ecuyer, believed that he was "collecting the forces of the horse in his centre in order to ease his extremities... The animal finds himself transformed into a kind of balance of which the rider is the centre-piece...The rider will know that his horse is completely gathered when he feels him ready as it were to rise from all four of his legs." (31).

Figure 27 The Rechargeable Battery

From my own experience I believe that I am collecting energy. I think of my horse with a huge rechargeable battery in his quarters. When I ride him in certain ways I collect energy in that battery. I recharge the battery and hold it there for future use.

Movements which create more energy then they expend are "collecting" movements. They include: work in confined areas; small circles; tighter turns; lateral work; downwards transitions; rein-back; counter-canter; approaching a fence; slower paces. The assumption here is that all the work is correctly executed. Incorrectly executed work achieves nothing.

This stored energy can be released from the battery intentionally to create powerful extensions. Movements which expend more energy then they create are "releasing" movements. They include: work in open spaces; straight lines/diagonals; faster paces; extended paces; landing from a jump.

Collecting Movements	Releasing Movements
Work in confined areas	Work in open spaces
Small circles (voltes)	Larger circles, work on the track
Tighter turns	Straight lines
Lateral work	Work on two tracks
Downwards transitions	Upwards transitions
Rein-back, pirouettes	Free walk on a long rein
Counter-canter	Extended canter
Approaching a fence	Landing after a fence
Slower paces	Faster paces, extensions

Energy can also be released unintentionally through leakage – usually, as with all batteries, through faulty connections. In the rider's case the connections allowing leakage are our seat and hands. Too weak a contact will leak energy. Too strong will block our ability to release energy.

Energy can also be wasted when we are not straight and streamlined. For efficiency we need the part in front of the engine to be aligned with it.

We can also waste energy when we go too fast. Pushing our horse forwards faster and faster is inefficient movement.

Have you felt this yourself? Correct extensions use energy that we have already accumulated. The feeling is that it is always possible. We simply allow it to happen. It looks effortless, and it is. In contrast incorrect extensions are fuelled on energy created in the movement – it looks full of effort, and it is. As Paul Belasik says in his book, Dressage for the 21st Century (7), "If nothing can be let out, nothing was being stored up".

The battery, essentially the horse's physique, grows stronger through training and so more able to create and contain larger amounts of energy.

So, just to summarise on collection. I believe that riding is about efficient movement. Movement requires energy. An effective rider generates energy; conserves it well; and uses it efficiently. She manages the horse's battery!

To ensure this energy is used efficiently it should not be blocked; it must flow freely through his body. So tension has an impact on impulsion. To avoid wasting energy we need our horse's body to be mechanically efficient. The term we use in dressage is straightness.

Straightness
The BD Rules Book 2006 states that "The aim is that the hind legs step into the tracks of the forelegs both on a straight line and on a circle, and that the rider has an even feel in his reins."

I think a better term for "straightness" would be "alignment". We often talk about straightness for the horse but it is very important for the rider too. Why is it important? It is important for efficiency; to achieve ease of movement. This is the effect in the short term. But there is a longer term need for straightness. Better alignment gives us more even wear and tear on the limbs. It helps to maintain soundness and therefore our horse's ability to sustain his performance in the longer term.

Can true straightness ever be achieved? Straightness is an ideal. It should be possible for a horse with perfect conformation but how many of those do we see? However, it can always be improved. How? To improve alignment we have to "decontract"; to remove excess tension. But this is chicken and egg because to let go we must be aligned – otherwise we will lose balance.

The horse must allow us to direct his available energy by accepting our contact; in the hand; the leg and the seat. For him to accept we must be acceptable. We must make ourselves as easy to carry as we possibly can by improving our own position (aligning ourselves and removing tension to the minimum necessary) and continuously softening ourselves to ensure we don't block him, anywhere.
Impulsion affects balance. Too much or too little can result in lost straightness and/or lost balance.

Our ability to straighten our horse is affected by the horse's conformation or his natural degree of straightness. And the degree to which he will allow us to do this.

We have already seen that tension (what's happening on the inside) affects straightness (what we see on the outside). One sign of straightness is tracking true. In other words, the hind prints follow in the same arc as the fore prints. Tension in the horse affects tension in the rider. A horse with a tense back is not easy to sit to!

What affects tension? Calmness in the mind and relaxation affect tension. Tension affects balance and therefore regularity. In turn, attending to the rhythm and keeping things the same is comforting for the horse. It calms him and reduces tension. He starts to breathe more deeply and regularly. One outward sign is relaxed snorting. Easier work, well within his capabilities, is also calming for the horse.

So far we have discussed the rider's impact from the point of view of her seat and balance and therefore her ability to impede her horse. We have also mentioned the rider's impact through training, fittening and feeding. An effective rider trains her horse to become responsive to smaller requests. If she is unable to do this she has to resort to force and physical strength. The more the rider uses force the more tense the horse will be, the less able he will be to move freely forwards and so the harder the rider will have to work. Good riding appears effortless for horse and rider because it is effortless. You do have a choice.

I have felt the effect of the variables and relationships both for myself and for my horse.

Take some time to consider how they have worked for you.

We can combine all these variables and relationships into a causal loop diagram shown in Figures 28 (horse) and 29 (rider). The diagram was created in a software package called Vensim (36). Variables which have been copied and appear elsewhere in a larger diagram are shown in grey in angled brackets thus: "<xxx>".

Starting on the right hand side with collection -The greater the degree of collection of our horse, the better his balance will be and the more he will move with ease and lightness. He will be able to maintain his balance and rhythm through increasingly difficult movements. Indeed, Inger Bryant explained that the test of whether the horse has sufficient collection in a dressage test is whether he can maintain his balance and rhythm for the movement in question.

Collection is affected by impulsion which is in turn affected by energy and alignment (straightness, mechanical efficiency). The horse's alignment is affected by the rider's alignment; the degree to which the horse allows the rider to influence him through the connection, and of course, his own conformation.

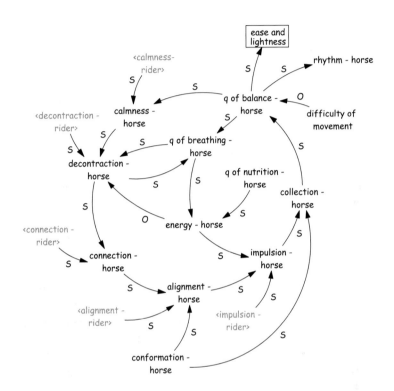

Figure 28 Scales of Training Inter-Relationships (Horse)

The quality (q) of the connection is affected by the decontraction of the horse and the quality of the rider's connection to him. I think that this is what we call "feel".

The horse's decontraction is affected by his breathing, his calmness, his energy level and the decontraction of the rider. The better the quality of breathing the more decontraction; the greater the decontraction the better the quality of breathing. Energy needs to be balanced with calmness. All other things equal more energy gives less relaxation. This is the great rider challenge; managing energy and maintaining decontraction. To improve decontraction, the rider must decontract herself and/or reduce energy levels. John Micklem always told me – never create more energy than you can control. This has implications for feeding too.

Calmness is the foundation on which everything else is built. Like us, when our horse feels challenged, shown physically by a loss of balance, he will tend to lose his calmness. As he becomes more able to maintain his balance in more and more difficult situations so his calmness will improve too. The rider has a major influence here. She must be calm herself and she must aim to manage her horse's calmness by working on the boundary of his comfort zone.

The same relationships are at work for the rider.

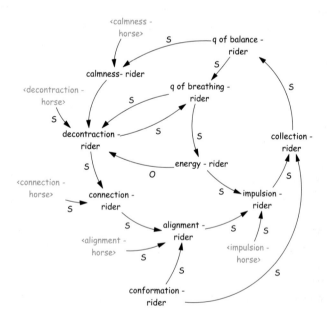

Figure 29 Scales of Training Inter-Relationships (Rider)

Can you describe the relationships in Figure 29? Have you experienced these relationships at work when you ride? How does what you have experienced differ?

The Way Forward

For the community of riders, trainers and judges to unite they need energy, and alignment to common objectives and values. This is the spirit of cooperation not competition. The foundation of cooperation is communication. And the foundation of good communication is clear unambiguous language. I applaud the Global Dressage Forum and its initiative to create agreed definitions of dressage terms. We can all contribute our views to this at the internet address in the appendix (28).

All language will be ambiguous to an extent. Ambiguities are often resolved when individuals discuss their mental models in a group and aim to capture their shared agreed understanding in a cause and effect diagram. At the end of the day it is our behaviour that demonstrates our true values much more than our words.

To improve we need to be able to share our understanding. This means that we must make it explicit so that we can challenge, understand and share. I have described my mental model of the relationships I believe are at work when I ride.

How do they fit with yours? How do they fit with your trainers? Your friends? The judge marking you in competitions?

I think that the best way forward would be to bring together a group of recognised and knowledgeable trainers (for example, the International Dressage Trainer Club, Global Dressage Forum, BD Convention) to share their understanding of the cause and effect relationships at work. That way a more holistic understanding can be developed and shared.

I can think of many similar examples of this type of gathering from my previous career. Admittedly they were mainly for the board members of a private enterprise or a single government department. The most memorable example was a working meeting I ran with the Harrier Support management group within the RAF.

At the workshop were representatives from the Harrier maintenance team who were responsible for keeping the Harriers airworthy. In addition there were representatives from the Navy and RAF. I helped them to share their understanding of the cause and effect relationships affecting airworthiness of the Harrier fleet, and developed a cause and effect diagram with them using Systems Thinking. We used this diagram to identify root factors and who influenced them. Together they agreed ways of working together appreciating their shared responsibilities and what each influenced. It is a very powerful approach. And very energising for all involved. The training groups from the horse world would also benefit from this approach.

Things to remember
Training is about building sustainable strength based on understanding. Correct musculature can only be developed from a deep knowledge of the variables impacting strength and how they inter-relate.
There is a need for a deeper shared understanding of sustainable training to unite the horse world (riders, coaches and judges).

---

8 Rider Dynamics

> *"All we have to use, when we sit on a horse and guide it, is our own body from the top of our head to the soles of our feet, and the volition that drives it.*
> *Before we can expect to control the horse we need a high degree of control of ourselves. Gaining this is our first responsibility."*
> *Richard Weis and Susanne Miesner (32)*

Riding involves our whole self. To do it well we need to use our body and our mind. So we have to learn about ourselves, about our body and mind to use them more effectively and efficiently.

Mind and Body

An effective mind is characterised by the following: strength (ability to think deeply); suppleness (ability to think broadly); calmness (clarity, consistency); confidence (trusts ability to make sound judgements); and awareness (ability to feel). Note that this is the same for all minds – our own and our horses! Our minds may have different potentials but in my experience few beings exploit the full potential of their mind. And of course the way we develop the mind will differ from the human to the horse...but *the qualities we aim to develop are exactly the same!*

Mind/Body characteristics	Rider development	Horse development
Strength	Mind: research, stimulation, Systems Thinking Body: Pilates, yard work	Lunging, in-hand work, schooling, jumping
Fitness	Mind: concentration Body: riding, swimming, walking/running, interval training	Hacking, interval training

Suppleness	Mind: studying different subjects Body: bending, stretching	Variety in work
Calmness, Relaxation	Meditation, Alexander Technique, swimming, rest, massage, treats	Natural life style, freedom, grazing, friends, rest, hacking competing
Confidence	Robust mental models, self belief, self control	Consistency, reassurance, leadership
Coordination	Pilates, swimming, dancing, golf	Pole and grid work
Body Awareness (posture)	Pilates, Alexander Technique, swimming – any activities developing balance	Training, being ridden well, comfortable tack

All these activities use energy. Our mind and body need quality fuel in the form of a well balanced diet and self control to ensure that this fuel is well utilised.

Brain control
Body control is obvious! Few people may acknowledge "brain control", but I know that it is essential for riding! The skills we need are the same as our body control skills. We must work on our ability to:
- empty the brain ie relax/calm it entirely;
- flex the brain between thinking and feeling ie balance it;
- strengthen the brain by developing thinking skills and cultivating a positive frame of mind

What I am aware of is that I can use my brain in different ways.

I can use my brain to **gather information and think** (what affects what; what happens if I do X or Y; what is the best way forward). I can also use it **to structure** what I have learnt so that I can **share** it more effectively. I used this brain mode a lot in my work as a business consultant.

I can use my brain to **store information** – often vast quantities. I know this because I taught myself to do this at school and university. Getting results was all about memorising huge quantities of information, so that was what I did! Today I mainly use this function to store what I might call "links" – where I can find more about a topic.

I can use my brain to influence my body – **to feel** how my weight is distributed and to **control my muscles**. Harris (20) states that we also **store "feels"** – our brain is capturing a video of what we have seen and felt at every point in our life!

I think that we can choose how we section our brain between these three uses. Storage space is taken up by whatever we are storing and the more we store the more we grow our storage capacity. The rest we can choose to use in either thinking or feeling mode and we can partition (not literally!) our brain between these two uses. When we ride we are mainly in feeling and body control mode. However, we also think and store. The partitioning is, say, 80% feeling and 20% thinking. Then when we are off the horse but thinking about riding in the evening the percentages change to say 20% feeling and 80% thinking.

Thinking enables us to make better decisions. Typically we have to think through options and consequences to make the right choices. When we think through consequences we simulate forward – this can create fear! For example, seeing something spooky in the ditch at the side of the road on a hack. If we think about it, in no time we will have a major accident in our heads and this will affect our feel and our body.

This is negative brain energy. Negative thinking switches us into defensive mode. We lack confidence. We expect the worst. Our horse is right to stop trusting us! Adopting a positive attitude means that we are aware of the possibility of potential bad consequences but we don't dwell on them. Instead we focus all our energy on making positive things happen. We can use this force, this power of positive thinking, in all areas of our life. But with horses it is invaluable!

We must not be negative when we ride. We must concentrate our brain activity on feeling, relaxing and positive beliefs. If we are unable to do this we must use distracting techniques for our brain. Talking to a friend or singing can help. I discovered that my riding improved in lessons when I stopped thinking about what I had to do and just did it and talked to my teacher about other things.

Inger Bryant told me that she uses the same technique both in her own riding and in her teaching. She partitions the brain into two parts; "front of brain" and "back of brain". The thinking goes on at the back. The horse can "read" (feel) what makes it into the front. This means that to avoid the self-fulfilling prophecy we must not allow our negative thoughts to pass into the front of the brain.

Inside vs Outside

The key tool in riding is our self - our body and our mind. We can't go out and buy a new self, because you and I are unique!

We all have the potential for more, but we often spend valuable time lamenting what we are, using negative energy, rather than slowly but surely building what we **want to be** using positive energy – teaspoonful by teaspoonful.

The television is full of programmes about "make-overs" - cosmetics, hairdos, clothes, surgery, diets and so on. Appearances are relatively easy to change! Fortunately for we riders our horse doesn't care about the way we look. He doesn't notice our greasy unfashionable hair; our podgy tummy, our unfashionable clothes...only in so far as they affect our attitude – how we feel inside!

How many programmes do we see on television about what's on the inside? Not many! Why? It takes a long time to change the inside – be it the inside of our mind or our body. But this is what will make the real difference to our riding and to our lives.

Many riding books focus on the way the rider looks on the outside – her position. But for me the most important thing is how it feels on the inside. When it feels right it will look right – believe me. Working purely on the outside just plasters over the cracks. It will never completely correct what is on the inside...and it will appear on the outside again.

It will feel right when you are balanced; relaxed and following the horse's movement (Museler (15)). So stop trying to make it look right and go for making it feel right.

It is the same with our horse. When we try to make it look right (ie we only change the outside) it will not be sustainable. Once again, for sustainable results we must forget the outside and work on the inside – the horse's balance, his relaxation and his attentiveness to our aids. When we have these three things his outline will be right. Don't believe me. Try it and see for yourself.

Don't get me wrong. I am not advocating abandoning mirrors, video cameras and eyes on the ground. They are an invaluable form of feedback from a different perspective. They help us to calibrate look and feel so that we can build trust in our feel. They are especially important whilst we are learning to improve our feel as our own internal feel system is often distorted by years of habitual poor body use.

Body control
We are all unbalanced. There, I've said it! The only difference is the degree of unbalance.

Like our horses, we all have one side that is stronger (and therefore tighter and more contracted) than the other and the other that is relatively less strong but often more flexible and stretchy. My right side is flexible and stretchy and my left side is tight and contracted. I feel like my left hip and my left shoulder are both pulled towards my waist by strong muscles around my middle. This means that when I ride my left seat bone often feels more wishy washy and indistinct on the saddle.

Many authors and riding instructors suggest correcting crookedness from the outside. "Lift your left shoulder". "Lower your right shoulder". I have tried pushing my weight to the left; pushing my waist left; raising my left shoulder; pressing my left heel down and so on. In my experience none of these kinds of corrections work for me. Nothing which operates on the outside alone works...in my experience, we have to work on the inside.

I believe that crookedness is a distortion of the outside caused by uneven muscle tension on the inside. In fact, crookedness and tension are chicken and egg. The more crooked we are the more tension will be needed in our muscles to avoid falling over. The more tense we become the more crooked we will be. And the more crooked, the more crooked! Like building a domino tower, if the base is crooked we will have to build-in the opposite crookedness higher up the tower to retain balance.

The crookedness is usually a symptom not a cause. If we want to permanently fix the problem we have to go to the root cause. This means that we have to regain softness on the inside first. This will then allow us to feel how we are out of balance and make the necessary corrections. Otherwise we will fall over or have to introduce tension again to stay erect.

What works for me is focussing on relaxing and letting go. Every 10 seconds I have to correct my seat in this way. Checking the evenness, and when it is uneven, releasing back down again and carrying my upper body. I breathe deeply and regularly to reinforce this. I breathe in to the back of my ribs and as I breathe out I think of letting go throughout my torso.

The head is heavy. It must be carried above the centre of gravity. Otherwise it can cause all sorts of contortions in the body below it. Try it now – let your head tip first left then right – where do you feel the effect on your body?

It's not just that we are right or left handed. We also have a preferred leg. Which leg do you use to kick a ball? And a preferred eye. It is the same for the horse. Notice which of his hind legs is stronger.

We can all become more even but it takes time. You will have to confront and stop yourself so many times. When your instinct is to reach out with your right hand; stop; inhibit the habit and use the left; it will feel weird at first but just do it. You'll have to really concentrate and think about how to do it but you will get stronger and more capable. Practice writing with your other hand a little every day; gradually you will improve your ability to write legibly with your "other" hand. But it takes time.

Also, practice horse activities from the off side including mounting and dismounting; tacking up, leading, and rugging up. It all helps. I did and at first it feels totally alien but repetition familiarises the movement.

It sounds hard to do this but believe me, as in all things, we humans will take the easy way out. "It's quicker to do it the other way"; "I don't have the time" are just some of the excuses you'll use. And they're true. However, we must prioritise this for our longer term good as well as our horse's wellbeing. Do we do things for ease now or for choice later?

Putting your hands on yourself can give important feedback. On or off the horse putting one hand palm inwards on the lower back can help you to relax and let go in that area. This is an area we often over tense when riding.

> *"Each rider will have a different set of postural imbalances and compensations, and it is therefore advisable that individual rider analysis and assessment is considered when attempting a corrective exercise regime"* Kate Fernyhough and Rhona Watson[21]

Back problems
It is noticeable that many of the people I know with horses have back problems. Some friends have had fusion operations to stabilise their lower backs.

Over the years I have suffered a lot with my back. I learnt a lot about complementary therapies due to my problem. I practised the Alexander Technique for seven years. I tried osteopathic treatment and physiotherapy, as well as sports massage. Finally, I had an MRI scan which revealed a severely degenerated L5S1 disc in my spine. This is the last disc at the base of the spine. I was offered a relatively new procedure - a disc replacement operation, in which a prosthetic disc is used to replace the faulty disc(s).

An alternative was to chose the more conservative approach. I decided that the operation was too risky. Now I work on my core strength. I started learning Body Control Pilates in January 2005 and now use modified Pilates exercises especially for people with disc problems. I have been practising Pilates, and have been sound, ever since!

Pilates
Pilates helps us to develop:
Core strength
Pelvic stability
Effective breathing
Coordination
Muscle control
Muscle tone.

It does not help us to develop cardiovascular fitness.

Body Control Pilates is remarkably effective - and medically-approved. It is of an holistic nature, being based upon a well-constructed philosophical foundation. Central to the Method is 'awareness of your own body' and each and every exercise is built around eight basic principles:

Relaxation	Concentration
Co-ordination	Centring
Alignment	Breathing
Stamina	Flowing Movements

By working on the deep architectural structure of the body, 'core stability' is achieved, and then maintained, through increasingly complex movement sequences. Specific problem-areas can be targeted by an exercise, always in relation to the rest of one's body.

Your body awareness is heightened by bringing together mind and body - Body Control Pilates literally teaches you to be in control of your body, allowing you to handle stress more effectively and achieve relaxation more easily.

To find out more, a good place to start is the Body Control Pilates website (23) and Emily Kelly's book (24).

When I practice Pilates I often get to a point where I feel great. My eyes soften and I am less aware of the divisions between individual objects in my sight. I am more conscious of feeling inside myself and less conscious of seeing or hearing things outside myself. When I look in a mirror at this point I can't see myself, only the room. I feel warm. I am conscious of the blood flowing through me right to the tips of my fingers and toes. I feel truly alive and a part of everything. I feel like I am melting into the ground - allowing myself to be supported.

Have you felt like this? Do you believe me?

Pilates helps to build both core strength and flexibility and that makes it great to support your riding. However, you must make sure that you use a balance of Pilates movements to achieve this! Stretches lengthen and relax tense muscles. Other movements use different muscle groups and therefore help to build strength. We need both!

I've learnt a lot from my Pilates experience. I've learnt to listen to my body. When I did this I found that it told me what it couldn't do and what it would like to do. I learnt that this didn't work well in classes where we were expected to follow a set programme. I prefer to practice in an environment where I can set the pace and choose the exercises and where I can get feedback and help when I need it from a trained teacher.

I also learnt that one class a week and nothing in-between was not sufficient. I tried setting time aside each day for practice but this was difficult to manage. Instead I started to think about the principles of alignment, breathing, engaging the core and releasing whenever I could. So, mucking out the stables, soaking my hay, I practise Pilates. Sometimes I find myself to be so stiff in a certain area that I feel the need to do some specific stretches there and then – so I do. Our horses do this for themselves all the time.

I started to experiment using Pilates principles on horseback and I found them to be very effective. An even seat, stretching in warm-up, coordinating my breathing with my riding and aids really improved the effectiveness of my aids. Releasing (letting go) as I breathe out can be used to allow the horse increased freedom in upwards transitions. Breathing out and engaging the muscles in the core helps to stabilise the body in downwards transitions.

I interviewed Kate Fernyhough and Rhona Watson, two Pilates teachers who apply Pilates specifically to riding. Their responses are given in Appendix 3.

Alexander Technique

"You translate everything, whether physical or mental or spiritual, into muscular tension." F.M. Alexander 1869-1955

"Mr. Alexander has done a service to the subject [of the study of reflex and voluntary movement] by insistently treating each act as involving the whole integrated individual, the whole psychophysical man. To take a step is an affair, not of this or that limb solely, but of the total neuromuscular activity of the moment, not least of the head and neck."
Sir Charles Sherrington 1857-1952, Neurophysiologist, Nobel Prize for Medicine 1932

The Alexander Technique was first developed in the 1890s by an Australian named Frederick Matthias Alexander. As a young and promising actor, Alexander faced a problem which risked ending his career - his voice would become increasingly hoarse during performances, until he could barely produce any sound at all. He consulted doctors, but they could not diagnose any specific disease or cause of the hoarseness. With no clear medical cause for his problem, Alexander reasoned that he might be doing something wrong when reciting, leading him to strain or "misuse" his own vocal organs. As his only resort was self-help, he decided to observe his way of speaking and reciting to see whether he could spot anything unusual and to find a solution.

What emerged from this experiment of several years was more than just a vocal technique. Alexander gradually realised that the functioning of the voice depended on the correct balance of tension in his entire neuromuscular system, from head to toe. Alexander developed his technique to encourage and maintain this balance through conscious attention and control, a technique which has become applicable to a wide range of problems and aims. In short, this balance was extremely important for overall coordination and many other functions, such as breathing, posture, freedom of the joints in moving the whole body, using the arms and hands for skilled activities, staying calm under pressure, and maintaining good overall health.

Gradually, as others noticed improved health and performance, he began to show his technique to those who came to him for help. From about 1894 onward, he had flourishing practices in Melbourne, and later in Sydney, until this teaching became his main occupation. A number of doctors referred patients to him, including Charles Bage, the Melbourne doctor he had once consulted for his voice trouble. Actors also flocked to him for help. In 1904, in order to gain more recognition for his Technique, and prompted by his friend JW Steward MacKay, an eminent Sydney surgeon, he moved to London, where he worked until his death in 1955.

"Instead of feeling one's body to be an aggregation of ill-fitting parts full of friction and dead weights pulling this way and that, so as to render mere existence in itself exhausting, the body becomes a

coordinated and living whole, composed of well-fitting and truly articulated parts."
Sir Stafford Cripps, Former Chancellor of the Exchequer

"When an investigation comes to be made, it will be found that every single thing we are doing in this work is exactly what happens in Nature where the conditions are right, the difference being that we are learning to do it consciously."
F.M. Alexander

What are some of the things I might learn through the Alexander Technique?

During your course of lessons, you can learn how to

- be poised and stand tall, without stiffness
- move gracefully and precisely, with greater ease
- be alert and focused, and calm at the same time
- be active and energetic, without excess effort or tension
- be more self-aware and coordinated from moment to moment so your effort is appropriate to the task at hand.

In this way, you can avoid discomfort and strain in your daily life and favourite activities, and prevent wear and tear on your body. In short, you can perform better and achieve more, while wasting less energy.

There is a lot more information on the website of the Society of Teachers of the Alexander Technique (30) and in books such as Michèle MacDonnell's "Alexander Technique" (25). Richard Weis (32) uses the Alexander Technique extensively in his work on dressage riding technique.

My experience
I studied the Alexander Technique with Gloria Pullen, herself a dressage rider and teacher of teachers of the Alexander Technique.

Whilst Systems Thinking is the key to conscious learning for the mind, I believe that the Alexander Technique is the counter part for the conscious control of the self.

You must also be aware of what it doesn't do. It does not build core strength and fitness. For this reason I recommend Pilates and a symmetrical fittening exercise involving rhythm and coordination such as swimming or cycling. If you are over-weight do consult your doctor and seek professional help with a weight reduction and fittening programme.

Pilates and the Alexander Technique are great for dealing with day to day stiffness and tension. Once you have learnt them you can use the techniques yourself when and where you feel the need. In contrast, physiotherapy, osteopathy and massage require the intervention of a specialist. They are invaluable for dealing with injuries and illnesses on the muscular-skeletal system. But at the end of the day no one will care as much for your body as you!

Having said that I do like to treat myself to a good sports massage every now and then. If I could afford it I would indulge myself much more often. Athletes have realised the benefits of massage as part of a total body regime. I wonder how many riders treat their horses to a massage but forget about themselves?

It takes time to learn body control and develop core strength and fitness. Start now and build these things slowly and sustainably.

In the appendix you will find more information on osteopathy and massage and how it can help the rider.

We all need to understand our own bodies. Notice things. Track the behaviour pattern. I feel a negative impact from activities like pulling soaking hay-nets out of buckets; lifting bags of feed; pulling up temporary fencing posts; and cold drizzly weather. I feel a positive impact from a hot power shower; massage, heat pads, and the heat of the sun.

What makes you feel worse/ better?

Nutrition for riding
For riding we must cultivate a healthy body. It is not the purpose of this book to cover this vast topic. There are many good information sources readily available and some are listed in the appendix.

Some simple guide-lines:
- ensure you drink enough water
- exercise regularly (walking, swimming and cycling are all good)
- get sufficient rest/sleep
- eat foods close to their natural state or unrefined
- eat at least 5 pieces of fruit and vegetables a day
- limit intake of caffeine, alcohol
- quit smoking
- maintain a healthy body weight.

Being fat or thin is no indicator of nutritional intake. Many fat and thin beings are starving, nutritionally speaking! We need a balanced diet for sustainable health. I have found that by caring for my horses myself, doing 20 minutes brisk walking per day, and eating sensibly, my weight stays fairly stable.

This applies for our horses too. Many owners I know pay more attention to the outside of their horses (because its visible – not only to them but to others too) and neglect the inside. The effect is cumulative.

Fitness for riding
Riding fitness is best achieved by regular riding. You get fit for riding by doing it, and not overdoing it, REGULARLY. As with all things, little and often is better than a once a week binge. Remember that lasting fitness is built slowly. Your focus needs to be on regularity and

integrating activities into your life – not seeing them as temporary additions.

When I came out to France I was not in a good shape. I was ill and had lost a lot of weight (5'7" tall and 8.5 stones). This had made me thin and weak. It took me about a year to slowly rebuild my physical strength. A slow but sustainable development of strength is what is required. Many people yoyo their weight with fad diets. They do not understand the root causes of their weight change and so are unable to manage their system. Use systems thinking to understand your weight and fitness and then manage it properly. We only have one body.

Things to remember
We must work to strengthen our body and our mind.
Build understanding of your body.
Build core strength.
Positive thinking is very powerful.
Change the inside and the outside will follow.
Create a better balanced body.
Manage your fitness and nutrition.
Aim for a healthy lifestyle.

---

9 Application - Riding in the moment

> *"A correct, independent, balanced seat; a sound knowledge of the theories behind the practices; good feel; good timing; a sense of rhythm; a clear, calm focussed mind; an ability to 'read' the horse's requirements; persistence; modesty but not false modesty"*
> *Andrea Hessay (34)*

In chapters 4 to 6 we looked at the theory. Now lets look at the practice. How we can apply what we have learnt in the riding arena.

A typical training session will be structured as follows: Dismounted preparation and assessment; warm-up; ridden assessment; "work"; and, cool-down. In some riding sessions we may choose to exclude some of the stages, often due to time restrictions. I believe it is essential to include the warm-up and cool-down phases in all riding sessions. Sometimes, given the time available, we don't make it to the work phase. The answer is to make more time available, or accept that we haven't got the time to fully work the horse. We can't ride for improvement based on our watch!

In this chapter we consider each of the training stages.

Dismounted preparation

My preparation often starts before I go to the stables. I will warm myself up with some Pilates (simple stretches eg roll downs, side rolls, leg stretches). In an ideal world I will lunge my horse before I ride him. Usually I connect the lunge rein to a head-collar without side reins but with my usual saddle and bridle. I secure the reins by twisting and threading through the throat-lash. I believe this gives a similar feel to an equilibrium contact on the bit (see chapter 5 for a discussion of rein contact). Sometimes I secure the stirrups and sometimes I let them hang at a height where they will not catch the horse's elbow. The stirrups then encourage the horse forward as they follow the rhythm of his movement.

I find that lunging in this way:

- allows the horse to warm up without any burden or shaping;
- let's me assess his attitude to work before I feel it;
- get's me warm too. I like to think about my breathing, alignment and connection with the ground.
- enables me to do up my girth slowly before I mount. I have a dressage saddle with long girth tabs and it is more difficult to change the girth mounted.

I focus on getting him loose and going forward in a stretchy shape, this means that when I get on he is already active and helps prevent me pushing too hard with my seat. It allows me to concentrate on just relaxing myself as he is already forwards and warm.

Thoughts on lunging
Besides a useful warm-up, lunging can be used as a training session in its own right. Many riders abandon lunging after the horse's initial backing and riding away, but by doing so they miss out on a wonderful training opportunity.

The equipment I prefer to use is as follows:
- Bridle with noseband and reins either secured or removed
- A simple snaffle bit. If I plan to attach the rein to the bit I prefer to use a single jointed happy mouth snaffle with cheeks
- Saddle and lunge roller over the saddle. Many lunge rollers are not well designed. I find that the pads pinch the horse's spine because they are never sufficiently wide enough. Using a roller over a saddle helps to mitigate this
- Leather side reins adjusted to be unrestrictive. The horse must choose to work into the contact and seek it. He will object to the restriction imposed by too short side reins, and free forwards movement is likely to be blocked
- A soft but substantial lunge rein
- A well balanced lunge whip
- Gloves

- A safe working area. This could be a lunge ring, but I personally prefer a larger area where I can move the circle around and introduce straight lines if I choose

All the work that I do ridden, I can also practice off the horse on the lunge. This allows the horse to understand and find his balance without my weight. And it allows me to see, and deal with the problem, from a different perspective.

I find that the following works for me when lunging:
- Consistent commands, especially the tone of voice used, for different requests
- Frequent changes of pace and direction
- If he doesn't listen bring him closer on a smaller circle
- If he goes too fast bring him closer (smaller circle). When he has a better balance and rhythm let him gradually back out
- Keep the hand/arm still, relaxed and soft
- Don't get into a pulling match with a fixed arm – if he comes against the hand give the rein and send him forward
- A forwards thinking hand is essential. I find that a feeling of the hand being 2mm in front of the movement is better than 2mm behind the movement (which blocks forward movement). You can twist your hand outwards ie thumb towards the direction of movement to reinforce this
- Handle the whip with care. Avoid sudden movements. Start with small movements and never hit the horse with the whip in anger. I often like to rest the whip against my hip. In this way the horses sees the whip as an extension of me
- If your horse is afraid of the whip desensitise him gradually by carefully running the whip over his body
- Concentrate on the horse's back end. I often focus on the muscles behind the saddle and really think of working them in my head
- Vary the work – the pace, the length of stride, the size of the circle, spirals in and out, transitions, use of poles
- An exercise I often use involves spiralling in to a smaller circle and then releasing him back out onto a larger circle. The spiralling engages the inside hind and collects the horse naturally. He has to

find a better balance on a smaller circle. Be sure not to block with the hand. On the larger circle the energy collected on the smaller circle is released.

If the horse is bent inwards more than the natural curve of the circle then either there is too much energy and/or the horse is blocked. To rectify, give the hand. This can often happen on the stronger rein. If the horse is bending contra the circle, send him forwards and give and take with the hand to encourage a better bend. When achieved, be quiet.

Observe the placement of the horse's feet. Where does he place each hind foot? Is he straight? How big is the stride? Change the rein. What is the pattern now?

Does he take the lunge rein out or does he fall in/refuse to bend on the circle? Is this the same on both reins?

If he falls in I think of a huge force coming out of me and pushing him away.

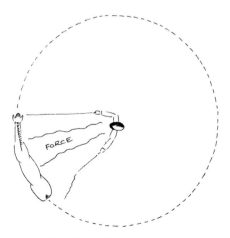

Figure 30 Lunging with the "Force"

I constantly remind myself not to use my hand but to leave it alone and relax it – when there is a problem I think of "The Force Outwards" and the movement forwards, reinforced with the lunge whip if necessary.

Many books warn us not to lunge in walk with side reins. I can understand the reasoning with short side reins but correctly adjusted unrestrictive side reins should still allow the natural movement of the head and neck in walk.

If it is not possible to lunge then it helps to "loosen" the horse prior to ridden work in some other way eg in a field or on a horse-walker. If neither of these is possible my warm-up includes a lot of walk and easy long low stretchy movements. I don't care whether the horse feels a bit sticky behind. I keep rising to the trot and try not to push too much – I just let him work himself warm.

Initial Assessment and warm up
For me assessing and warming up the horse go hand in hand. At the beginning of each and every training session with our horse we must stand back and make an assessment of what we have to work with. This assessment includes the way our horse looks and feels, and also very importantly, how we feel.

It is very important that when we do this we have NO EXPECTATIONS! We are totally in assessment mode – discovering what is – how do we feel – how does our horse feel – being honest but not being critical. And staying balanced – things are never all bad or all good! It is useful to give words to what we see/feel. For example, he feels full of excitement today, he feels tight through the shoulders, I feel tight in my right shoulder and neck, etc.

Whether I had lunged or not my ridden warm-up will be as quiet and calm as possible. The objectives are to:
- Warm up muscles
- Assess myself and the horse
- Start to work on the basic ingredients

- Establish a basic balance by work on my seat. This could include riding without reins, exercises and stretches on horseback, releasing in rising trot, minimising the rise, switching between rising/sitting/ standing for a given number of strides. I call this work "lunging myself". It is essential that the horse maintains a quiet rhythm and that the rider feels "safe" to do this well
- Stretch to release unwanted tension. Larger circles in trot or canter with a big inside bend help the horse to release through his shoulders. It is important that the rider is consistent with the stretch and keeps the contact as straightness is resumed. Just throwing the rein away or non-stop giving and taking can be very irritating to the horse.

It can help to talk to your horse about what you are feeling either aloud or in your mind. Apologise to him for not being soft enough yet or straight enough or whatever – but not desperate – just "forgive me, I'm working on it!" In return we have to do the same for him.
Canter can help to really loosen the horse and the rider. The key thing is just to let it happen. Let the horse's back move yours. Transitions in and out of canter will build energy but be careful with the excitement!

Charles de Kunffy, in his book, The Athletic Development of the Dressage Horse, (17) explains that walk and canter are the most natural paces for the horse. They are the paces our horse chooses most often when at liberty in the field. Recognise this and use this in your warm-up.

Go and watch top riders warming up at competitions. You will see some very different approaches. Recently I benefited from a visit to Saumur in France for an international dressage competition (CDIO***). I watched the warm-up for the Freestyle Grand Prix Music test. At one end of the scale I watched a French Cadre Noir rider on an Anglo-Arab preparing for his test with a very typical slow-build warm up - lots of slow work in walk with lateral work on a fair length of rein. Then slow stretchy trotting on the same lines. Then canter work, increasing engagement, and down to serious work.

At the same time a Portuguese rider commenced his warm-up with canter work in a collected outline. Shortening the canter, and going on again. Then pirouettes and changes. Poor execution was repeated. Good executions were rewarded with much verbal praise and patting with a period of walk on a completely loose rein. Whilst both warm-ups appeared to have the same underlying average level of energy and difficulty the actual patterns of energy were completely different.

I don't think that this means that we need to choose one of these methods. Rather we can learn by thinking through why the riders chose these particular ways of warming up. Some elements we may learn could help us but copying for the sake of it without understanding is rank stupidity!

Many riders wonder how long they should spend warming up. The answer is as long as it takes. Sometimes the whole training session could be just warming up!

Down to work
When you and the horse are warmed up you will feel that you are ready to do more.

Often at this point the missing ingredient is attention and focus, so I find that after warming up and loosening in all 3 paces it is useful to return to what I call "Pilates" for horses. This work is in walk. It gives both horse and rider time to concentrate, prepare and think about their balance. Exercises will include transitions between lateral movements – eg on a square; one side, shoulder-in; next side, travers; then shoulder-in etc. Leg-yielding along the wall. Walk-halt-walk transitions. Sometimes with rein-back. Frequent changes of direction. Frequent changes of frame eg from a square in lateral work to going large in free walk, change rein, commence square again.

I find that this work connects, controls and engages the horse's brain and hind legs and invariably I find him seeking my hand. It does the same for the rider. The need to "align and release" before and after each transition is good for me. The lateral work collects energy that is released in the active forwards work of free walk and straight lines. The effect is calming and harmonious and works with all types of horses and riders. Fizzy horses calm-down and concentrate, more laid back ones create energy with less effort! It is rewarding to all.

Some riders say that walk work switches their horses off. I can imagine that walk work without a pattern could do this but effectiveness in this exercise depends on the frequency of change. The rider must not switch off either!

I find that lateral work, performed in this way, collects energy in the horse. We saw in Chapter 7 how we need to collect energy and use it efficiently when we ride.

This is why we use collecting movements before we extend (or develop) a pace. Examples:
- Shoulder-in prior to medium strides on the diagonal
- Small circle before medium strides on the long side

Bringing the horse up - Changing the outline
We can't bring the horse up by hauling with our hands! The horse's head and neck come up as his whole posture changes, to enable him to balance...you can best see this on the lunge when we spiral the circle in. To balance, the horse will have to shorten his frame and raise his head and neck. A small circle, well executed, will always have this effect. Once the neck is "up" the rider can adjust her reins to maintain the same feel as before on a shorter rein.

How does the horse know to retain this outline when we move out of the small circle? The rider maintains the same feel through her seat! The old classicists call this "bracing the back" but basically it is about controlling the pelvis. Allowing less energy to flow through forwards, whilst maintaining the same total energy level, gives more up!

Consistency

The process of assessment, deciding what to work on, intervening and reassessing now commences. It is very important to be consistent throughout.

Consistency means being disciplined and sticking to the rules of correction and reward. Correction is often repetition or a stronger aid. Reward can be praise or maybe a break and a stretch.

It is about knowing when to be tougher...and having the confidence to be clear. If there is no physical reason that the horse cannot do as you are asking it is better to make a large and deliberate correction and then give. Ignoring the problem does not make it go away.

The subject of developing exercises to tackle certain desired improvements has been well covered by other authors. For completeness I have enclosed a few exercises that I have found work well for me, and which I use a lot:

Re-balancing:
Reduce pace (eg trot to walk); circle; half-halt; on lunge – smaller circle.

Increasing engagement of hind legs
Transitions; circle; shoulder in; leg yield; rein-back; work with poles.

Improving extensions
Increase engagement; prepare through collection.

Freeing tight shoulders
Big stretch on a circle (giving with outside rein); Spanish walk; spiralling.

Freeing hinds
Leg-yield along the wall, giravolta (see Paul Belasik "Dressage for the 21st Century (7)).

Increasing attention
"Pilates" work in walk, transitions, work in hand.

Increasing impulsion
Transitions; canter; alternating work and stretch.

Improving quality of transitions
Anticipation by using the same place to ask for the transition; wall;
circle.

Straightening
Shoulder-in, circles.

Better straight lines
Ensure adequate energy collection then release it towards a fixed point.

Calming
Meditation (long periods standing still); quiet work in walk; stretching in
trot.

Suppling
Changes of rein; shallow loops; circles; serpentines; varying outline –
stretching with nose still on/in front of vertical and not below shoulder
height.

Forward and down
The Shoulder-In volte (see Theresa Sandin's website (16) for a full
explanation of this); use of corners.

Up
Correctly executed downwards transitions; spiral in on a circle; adopting
a controlling seat (engaging the clutch). The horse's head comes up as he
changes his whole posture – this creates a loop in the rein that we can
remove without changing the feel in our hand.

> *Exercise:*
> *Choose a set of movements eg 10m circle, shoulder-in, halt etc. Then research and answer the following questions for each movement:*
> *How to get it right?*
> *What it does for the horse?*
> *What it does for the rider?*
> *What other movements it would help to prepare for?*

Training opposites
In each session we will find that we have to continuously re-establish a balance between seemingly competing objectives. The right balance gives us a harmonious outcome. The wrong balance is never so.

The key balances I have found myself working with are:
- Calmness vs energy
- Straightness vs bending
- Forwards vs sideways/backwards
- Collected vs extended paces
- Strength vs flexibility
- Down vs up
- Frame lengths
- Introducing new exercises vs confirming old ones.

We always have choices to make on each "balance". For example, if he's calm but lazy how do I create more energy but retain calmness? I could choose to simply inject more energy and sacrifice calmness temporarily before re-establishing it. Or I could seek ways of creating extra energy without losing calmness – "putting it in teaspoonful by teaspoonful". Do we overshoot and try to re-establish an equilibrium or do we gradually seek an equilibrium?

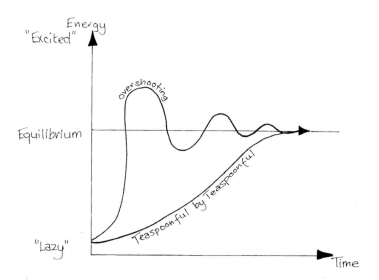

Figure 31 Seeking an equilibrium – choices of route

Exercises can be used to establish building blocks or as an end in their own right. In a dressage test before a judge all our movements are ends. In the warm-up before the test, we are working on establishing the building blocks on which the success of our test is built. It is important to be clear about why and how we are using each exercise. Is it to create balance or to prove it?

Cool-down
Aim to finish each session on a positive note.

It is important to allow time for the horse to cool down after work. If he has access to a paddock you could turn him out. If not, be sure to cool down with plenty of walk on a long rein in the arena. Or dismount and finish as you started with stretchy work on the lunge. Alternatively, this could be a good time for you and your horse to go for a walk together in the countryside. You could ride, but I think it's nicer for you both to walk together.

After I have done Pilates I like to massage or slap my tired muscles to increase circulation. I do the same for my horse when I remove the saddle. I massage and slap the area underneath and behind the saddle. Ideally I also like to turn the horse out afterwards for him to stretch his muscles and massage his back himself by rolling.

Some thoughts on riding exercises
Stopping

Like cars, some well schooled horses have brakes which are very sharp and respond to the lightest touch, whilst others require more effort. To halt just stop following the movement of the walk with your seat – this can be done sharply for an immediate transition, or gradually. Inwards pressure down the thigh to the knee, without losing the seat, can reinforce the request. If the horse doesn't respond to this polite request we must resort to the hand. After a few repetitions he should have the message that it's nicer for you both to halt from the seat.

Assess the quality of the halt from the feel in your seat. Does one seat bone feel higher than the other? If so, the hind leg on the lower side has been "left behind". Try to correct by a "nudge" with your seat bone on that side.

Going

To move off from halt into walk use as little effort as possible. Ideally it is releasing because there should always be the possibility of move off, so just a small nudge with the seat should suffice. Some horses require a lot more than this, especially before they are warmed up. Try a nudge with the leg as well as the seat movement, then the whip and your voice. With many repetitions you should be able to do less and less and the horse should still understand.

Once we have our horse responsive to our aid to move forward we can be more particular. It is possible for the rider to select the hind leg to commence the move off. To do this decide which hind you would like to step forward first in the move-off and start the sequence of the walk with your seat on that side.

> *Test your control by riding on an inner track. Can you ride a straight line in walk without the support of the track? Do nothing. What happens? Try it again? What could you try to correct?*

Turning
Turning should not need much effort from the rider.

Try this exercise. In an enclosed school simply ride the horse towards the corner – most will turn naturally using a quarter 10m circle. Sit square to the movement, there is no need for excessive movement of legs, hands or upper body. Notice how the horse turns on each rein. Think "how could I help him?" In the corner; inside knee. Before the corner slight turn of upper body, then release and allow horse to go through the corner. Successful turning is all about setting it up, then letting it happen.

Turn comes from your body not your hands. It requires a combination of inside and outside aids – seat check – weight into inside seat bone and outside heel (still 50% of weight each side – constantly check this).

Test the effect of turning only from the inside aid or the outside aid then both together. What happens? What have you learnt? Try turning with your hands alone. What happens?

Try circles of different sizes. How do you need to adjust your weight to achieve them? Combine the turning with the halt, move-off and stride length variation.

Circles
Circles are brilliant!

The perfectly shaped circle is the only movement with the possibility of total consistency. Absolutely no change – the same, the same, the same. Circles are great for developing acceptance and calmness, and developing rhythm to achieve a sustainable equilibrium:

- They collect the inside hind leg. They teach the joints to bend more. The smaller the diameter of the circle the more bending of the joints and the quicker the steps need to be
- They engage the outside hind leg and teach the horse to take a bigger step
- They strengthen the inside musculature (contracting muscles)
- They stretch the outside musculature (extending muscles)
- They slow the speed naturally (all other things equal) and so help to rebalance the horse
- They help us teach the horse the lateral aids
- They help us to teach the horse the aids to use a positive inside hind.

To achieve the full benefit of circles it is important that they are ridden accurately. Circles are traditionally thought of in terms of quarter circles. That is to say, fix 4 points and then ride a smooth turn between them. A straight line between them would create a square. In actual fact a true circle consists of an infinite number of points.

Transitions
The only constant should be change. Change the length of the stride in all paces. Practice transitions such as walk-halt-walk and halt-reinback-walk.

Going sideways
Lateral movements, such as leg yielding, shoulder-in and travers, engage the inside hind leg and lift the horse into your hand.

Lateral movements should be effortless. Ask yourself how you can do it with less. Turn as though you will change the rein, then as the horse starts to leave the track send the energy down the track. Always look where you are going.

You can practice lateral movements on the track or on an inner track. The track will help you to establish your lateral work. Once established, it should be the same whether executed on the track or away from it.

Leg yielding facing the wall is an excellent exercise for both rider and horse. The horse has to be "in your seat" (connected) and light in your hand. Cut off the corner, release, release, legs long, weight into toes, let it happen, be stable, light and allowing, carry your upper body. If you become stuck simply ride out of it and release – don't try to correct if you have lost it as you will fiddle and fiddle and fiddle! And you will become tighter and tighter and tighter in your body.

We have to stop trying with all our will to "do the exercise". Instead, just think. Think minimum and believe it will happen. Balance, and release, to allow it to happen. If it goes away don't interfere and fiddle to try to get it back – just ride away and think release – give in the whole body and then just come again. Think about your breathing. Breathe in deeply. This affects the whole body and alleviates stiffness by stretching muscles. Let go as you breathe out............concentrate, connect.

Going backwards
This is an excellent exercise for energy collection.

When teaching the young horse it is useful to start this exercise on the ground. A push on the shoulder with "and back" is usually enough to initiate a few steps. Reward the horse.
Later, the same can be done with an assistant on the ground when you are mounted. The rider helps the horse with her seat. Soon the horse will respond to the rider's voice and seat. And ultimately the seat alone. This can be reinforced by repeating the exercise at the same place in the school.

Rein back can be an important precursor to halt-trot and halt-canter transitions. The energy collected for the rein-back can be utilised for the move off into the quicker paces. It helps the rider to understand and emphasise the change in the seat from rein back (pelvis tilting slightly forwards) to the "up and on" of a move off to trot or canter (pelvis changes to tilt slightly forwards).

Improving the Canter
I was told I couldn't canter and believed it!

To get the feel of the canter we have to learn not to do anything except carry ourselves. So commit to the transition - upper body back, hand not blocking, then go with it, go with it, just carry yourself and feel what happens to your seat – don't do anything – just feel.

From – "Don't let him do that", "I must get this right" to "What happened then? Why? It doesn't matter. Let's have another go………". Riding is a learning process …..you must enjoy the learning to enjoy riding.

I used to think that my horse was judging me and finding me wanting. I was scared of this – I was also scared of hurting the horse. Inevitably the horse will be uncomfortable by us sitting on him – we have to accept this – otherwise we shouldn't ride him!

The quality of the canter will follow the quality of the transition and the quality of the preceding pace. The best way to improve the canter is not by cantering for long periods. It is through transitions. There are many possible transitions to canter:
- Walk to canter
- Trot to canter
- Rein-back to canter (helps to train halt to canter)
- Halt to canter
- Giravolta to canter. Giravolta is essentially a protracted turn on forehand (see Paul Belasik's Dressage for the 21st century (7))
- Leg yield to canter – either from a circle or a straight line or towards the wall.

The degree of difficulty of the strike-off increases depending on "location" as follows:
- approaching corner
- on a circle

- on the track (from shoulder/fore for greater ease. I find it better to think I am about to do a corner)
- on $\frac{3}{4}$ line (from shoulder/fore for greater ease – really telling!)

Why canter? What we hope to achieve by cantering can best inform us how to make the transition. For me the transition to canter is very important and it is easier to get a balanced transition and retain a connected seat from the walk. Think tall; allow the inside seat bone forwards and down; give with the hands; allow your horse forward through your seat. Ensure that your feet are underneath you so that you can keep a lighter seat.

If your leg is more in front of you all the weight is in your seat and passes directly into the horse's back. As a result the horse hollows his back making it uncomfortable for you to sit to; you tense and then the problem gets worse. A vicious cycle!

If your leg is too far back, you will tip forwards with your upper body to compensate and this will push your weight onto the horse's forehand. Like this he will find it very difficult to strike-off into canter and once in canter, if this occurs, he is likely to fall out of canter as he is pushed onto his forehand.

With the leg directly underneath we can carry more weight into the thigh ie your weight is supported over a larger area. This means less pressure per square inch on the horse's back and more comfort for the horse AND for you. Whatever you do, don't tense up! Focus forwards, sit up, release and give the hand forward.

I have really struggled with my seat in canter over the years. I have discovered a number of ways of improving my seat in canter:
- Lots of walk - canter - walk transitions on a circle
- Figure of eight in canter with simple change
- Thinking of growing tall, releasing, releasing, releasing the weight of the body on the thigh and equal weight into left and right of seat

- Legs long. Think of legs being pulled down by a force. Most people are not open enough behind the knee and in the ankle joint. Oil those joints
- Downwards feeling from centre down – upwards feeling from centre up. Try to make a space between each vertebra
- Let the body innards just be. Let them go where –ever they want to go, but don't hold on to any of them.
- Distract your busy mind by counting strides.

> *Try the following stride counting exercise. Commence a 20 metre circle in trot; transition to canter; canter a set number of strides (say 5) then trot; then repeat. Allow the horse into trot; feel the moment where he becomes more secure in your hand and keep allowing him forwards in the trot. It is very important that balance is maintained through all this.*

With a good canter seat you can execute many movements in canter. For example, shoulder in, counter canter. Try changing the frame in canter but be careful! As you ask for stretching down, the weight on the forehand increases and the horse could fall out of canter. You will need to support him with your seat to stop him going faster and losing his balance.

Training counter canter – Michel Henriquet (10) and Paul Belasik (7) have different ideas. Try both and see what works for you.

Improving the canter – the canter must "jump". Aim for bigger, longer more purposeful strides, not short and "on the spot". Trot, canter, trot transitions can help with this. Also try using canter poles – single and multiple.

Improving the Trot
We must start with the end in mind. What needs to be improved? Is it something you can feel or see (eg on the lunge)? Is there any difference between the trot loose, on the lunge, ridden? Does he have a naturally good trot? Is the need for improvement more visible in certain trot variants ie working, medium, extended, collected. How does he compare

to other horses you ride or see working? How would you describe the symptoms you see or feel? What do you think are the possible causes? Until we fix the root cause we'll not fix the problem, we'll just mask it. A good way of tracing root causes is to ask why 5 times or even more.............and you need to be really honest.

The consensus among trainers is that trot is an easier pace to improve than canter; but only within the individual horse's limitations. To do this we need to encourage the horse to push more from behind. The hind leg needs to carry more weight so that the forehand can lighten, and the trot becomes "more uphill".

This is easier said than done, particularly with a young horse (and even more so with a big young horse) as they easily lose their balance. Often the answer becomes more leg, but this just increases the speed and the horse becomes more and more unbalanced and leans on the hand. It is a bit like a child running down hill faster and faster - more and more unbalanced - and a lot of tears at the bottom. To engage the hind leg we often need to slow the trot and give with the hand. Whenever he dives onto the hand and quickens, slow him again and give with the hand (a long-as-needs-be half halt). You will really need to support him with your body and particularly the strong spring in your lower back.
Generally, I don't "work" the trot until I've cantered. First of all I warm up in walk and trot on a relatively long rein - concentrating on forwards and bending (corners, circles). I encourage him to listen to me through lots of transitions. The canter loosens me and him and gives "spring". Canter, trot, canter transitions on a 20m circle with a very light hand and concentrating on being as quiet as possible. I agree with Kyra Kyrklund (18) that the best trot comes after a good canter-trot transition, and the best canter after a good trot-canter transition.

Smaller (10m) circles help to engage the hind leg; really think about the inside hind on the circle and feel you can suck it up and under - then go large and try to keep the same feeling of the trot on the smaller circle but without using the rein - just your body. On the circle, check you aren't blocking or holding on the inside rein by smoothly giving it - the outline and the circle shouldn't change..........

In transitions (walk-trot-walk; halt-trot-halt), the rider must be soft and connected, especially in her seat and hands. The horse seeks the contact. The rider only carries the weight of the rein plus an ability to feel the horse. Downwards transitions develop collection, the carrying capability of the hindquarters, and balance. Upwards transitions develop engagement, the pushing capability of the hindquarters, and strength.

Shoulder-in down one half of the long side then straighten and release through your seat to gradually extend the contained power of the shoulder in. Or use the power to create true straightness and purpose across the diagonal. Remember, you need to carry yourself evenly and look at something at eye height in the direction you are going. Ride a small circle before the shoulder-in to really help. Balanced extension can only come out of collection. The feeling should be of releasing the contained energy that is already there, rather than creating it in that moment or "making him do it". You should feel that it is there for you all the time as you have created it with all the previous work.

The hand must give all the time, it should never block, as then the hind leg cannot come under and the back can't swing. Make good use of the rising trot....but remember you can still block with your body and hands in rising trot - stay relaxed, in balance and giving.

Keep varying the pace in the trot - forward and back. For example, contain it on the long side - release and lengthen a little through the corners and short sides.

You should be able to vary the outline too. In a long and low outline our horse is never behind the vertical. His nose should be level with his shoulders and no lower. This gives sufficient stretch. Remember to control the transition between outlines and don't let him dive down. Use the seat before shortening the rein - make it smooth - practice and practice. Do it by feeling, not by thinking about it. You need to be in a really calm, quiet, confident place in your head for this to work. This is not about control, it's about communication.

I have been experimenting with the use of poles on the ground - both on the lunge and ridden. They add interest and variety. They help to maintain attention. They make the horse aware of his movement pattern. He must think about how he can use his legs in different ways. Poles can be used to help de-contract the horse. The rider should stay in balance, relax and allow. Poles can also be used to train the horse to trot in different ways. Over time the rider can associate the feeling over the poles with a difference in her seat. The idea is for the feeling over the poles to be recreated without poles, at will.

Tracking up
Tracking up can be an indicator of engagement. However, conformation is a big factor here. Also, it tells us nothing about collection or extension. Paul Belasik (7) concludes that to truly determine stride length we have to measure actual length of stride.

Developing the Whole
Vary the work to keep both you and your horse interested. Many non-dressage riders talk about "boring" circles. The truth is, dressage should never be boring for the horse but it will be if the rider is bored. If you are bored do something different. But don't use this as an excuse to neglect your horse's education.

The type of work will vary depending on the purpose of the session:
- Obedience - training
- Fittening - training, hacking
- Muscle building - collected work
- Suppling
- Educating (broadening experience and horizons) - hacking, travelling, competing, taking your horse for a walk
- Assessing - lessons, competing

Riding should be fun for you and your horse. I have noticed that whenever I am looking forward to my riding I ride well. In contrast whenever I am riding because I feel that I should I don't ride very well.

Have you noticed the same thing? What affects you looking forward to your riding?

Going with the flow
Who says we should work our horse for exactly one hour each day? Often at exactly the same time each day. Try adopting a more flexible approach...listening to your body and your horse's body. Some days this may mean you ride for an hour. Some days you may not ride at all. Others you may ride for 30 minutes or for two 40 minute sessions, whatever feels best for you and him. The point is that you choose and know why you made that choice.

Training and competition
Are training and competition compatible?

A friend of mine explained that she won't compete because of how it changed her behaviour and compromised her riding in her desire to win. She felt this happening both at the event and in the last few weeks leading up to the event. The message is that competition is bad.

I don't have the same point of view. Competition is fine as long as we do not behave competitively, and allow that to compromise our principles of training. Top riders on teams must feel the need to achieve NOW at all costs but we ordinary riders don't have this pressure given to us – *we choose to place it on ourselves.*

The pressures of competition are undeniable. However, we can all make a choice about how we respond to these pressures. I feel that if we know that we can't make good choices when faced with these pressures, then it is better not to put ourselves in that situation. If, however, we do feel an ability to make good choices for ourselves, and our horses, then I think that competition can be enormously rewarding and an educational experience for both horse and rider. Competitions are an opportunity to gain important feedback on our training and its future direction.

I'm not saying that I can do this. I'm just saying that this should be possible. I think we all know well the negative aspects of competition but there are some positives too - balance in everything eh?

What do you think?

Things to remember
The way you feel before your ride will influence the quality of your riding so don't forget your dismounted preparation.
Lunging is a valuable way of warming up, assessing and preparing the horse before riding or instead of riding.
Warming up and cooling down are vital components of every training session.
Assess what the horse, and you, need in the moment. Avoid mechanically repeating the same exercises in the same places.
Feel, diagnose, choose a suitable exercise, try it, feel the response.
Commit to understanding the movements in your head – not just how to do them but what they do for you and the horse. Only then can we make the best use of movements.
Work in all 3 paces to develop the whole.

10 Managing your performance

> *"Be realistic ...Learn to ride properly ...Find a good trainer...Get yourself sufficiently fit ... Try to ride, or have your horse ridden, regularly ... Go to as many seminars, conferences, clinics ...discuss, argue, read, watch, do" Andrea Hessay (34)*

For the last 20 years I have worked at the forefront of international Performance Management consultancy. Horses have been my passion but business has been my career.

It seems to me that there are some interesting parallels between the business manager and the dressage rider:
- Both are centres of control, communication and guidance.
- Both represent an additional "weight" that the other party (the horse or the organisation) has to "carry".
- Both need to manage with understanding, clarity, tact, empathy and fairness to bring out the best in their partners and add value to the whole.

Just like the dressage rider, in order to succeed a business manager has to have:
- clear achievable goals
- strategies to achieve these goals
- an understanding of the complexity – the multitude of cause and effect relationships leading to achievement or failure
- a balanced holistic view
- the ability to tactically manage performance in the short-term with a watchful eye on sustainable long term results
- focus on the right things; continuous monitoring and intervention to improve when necessary with an understanding of the likely consequences of intervention
- flexibility
- an interest in continually learning about what makes the business tick and adapting techniques from other fields
- partners aligned to goals and values achieved through communication

- the ability to involve, motivate, reward and correct in an informed
and balanced way.

Whether we are aiming to create a high performing organisation or a
high performing dressage partnership the fundamentals are the same.

Finding the right horse
I see so many of my friends struggling with equine partners that don't
suit them.

They often have:
- horses that are too big for them;
- horses that are too much for them;
- horses that are not built for soundness;
- horses that cost a lot of money (both to buy and keep).

We often go for the horse we think we should have rather than the
horse we really want.
 "I need a big horse to fill the judge's eye";
"All talented horses have a catch";
"He has worked at Grand Prix – I need a schoolmaster to teach me";
"It's only one leg that is bent";
"I work hard, I deserve it"

I have found that...
The more money a horse costs, and the higher the level he has worked
at before, the more pressure on you.

The bigger the horse the more he will cost to keep and the more
difficult he will be to ride.

The poorer the conformation the more the horse will be prone to injury
and unsoundness and the less you will get to ride him.

The more nasty the horse is in the stable the more you will expect from
him when ridden and the more disappointed you are likely to be.

What have you found?

Does size matter?

Big, or should I say, tall, horses have become very popular in competition dressage. Why is this? Is it necessary? Is it even an advantage? Klaus Ferdinand Hempfling (19) believes that "a horse intended for a person 5ft 7in tall should measure between 14.1hh and 15.1hh. For a person 5ft 11in tall the horse's height should be between 14.3hh and 15.3hh." I am 5ft 7in. Why did I always feel embarrassed riding my 15hh Arab in competitions?

Take a look at photographs in books. Paul Belasik looks fabulous on his grey Andalusian "Exelso" in "Dressage for the 21st century" (7). Do you think that Exelso looks too small for him? Does Mr Belasik look better or worse on the other, larger, horses portrayed in the same book?

Olivera (8) was not a small man. Yet he rode many small horses. The partnerships could not be improved by horse size alone...

My partner is a cyclist. Serious cyclists are obsessive about their bike fitting them and have bikes designed with geometry to suit their individual conformation. I find this very interesting. Perhaps it is the same for the rider? Riders come in very different shapes and sizes. Perhaps we need to bear this in mind when we look for our equine partner and aim to find a horse that better matches our own conformation. After all, we can't change that!

The perfect horse

I'm not saying there is a perfect horse, for there is no such thing. But I think there is an ideal horse for each one of us, where the balance of positives and negatives works for us. In other words we can accept the problems. In my experience it's whether we can live with the down side that defines the sustainability of a relationship.

What qualities do you appreciate in horses? Why?

My old horse, Shantie, is a head-shaker. I didn't know it when I bought him. I certainly didn't like it and wished I could change it for him as well as for me. But I couldn't. And no amount of anguish and "miracle cures" worked. Eventually I learned to live with it and see it as a part of him. Someone else may not have felt this way. He may have been passed from owner to owner and probably have ended up at the knacker man relatively early in life.

The same horse also has a club foot. I guess that technically he is a disabled horse. But because he is a horse nobody ever told him about his disability! He just got on with his lot and achieved an amazing amount. This was the first horse I bought myself. I loved the way he looked – Shantie is a 15.1hh Palomino Part-bred Arab. He floated over the ground and jumped like a stag. He is the most forward thinking sensitive little horse I have ever sat on. Ignorance was bliss!

My friends told me he was too small for me (I'm 5 ft 7ins). They told me not to waste time on a head-shaker. They told me I deserved better. I knew different. I loved and still love and appreciate him!

Since Shantie I have bought 3 more horses. I bought Penny, a 4 year old 15hh Trakehner cross thoroughbred mare, with a friend (my riding teacher). She was unbacked and going cheap at a local dealer. I bought her as an experiment to understand how horses were backed and trained initially. I never thought of her as "mine". My friend eventually bought my share of the mare for her daughter.

The big mistake I made was buying a horse I will call J. A 16.1hh 6 year old Chestnut Irish Sports Horse gelding with 65 BD points. He was a "dressage horse". I had a video of a professional dressage rider schooling him in a beautiful outline to prove it. I tried him several times, including out for a hack in the woods when the owner was bucked off her other mount and broke her finger. J did nothing. The owner assured me he would be perfect for a novice aspiring dressage rider such as me. More than that she said she would help me if I had problems with him (and I believed her). The vet gave him a clean vet's certificate. My riding instructor rode him and said if I didn't buy him she would. The owner gave me a written warranty for soundness and temperament.

Everything told me he was ok except one thing; my intuition. With other horses, I had known straight away that they were for me. I didn't with J. He ticked every box in the logic stakes and this meant that I was looking for something wrong, a concrete reason to discard him. But there were none, except this nagging doubt inside me. I doubted but went for it anyway. I didn't have much experience buying horses and put it down to this.

I regretted it immediately. He was rearing as I led him for the first time towards the riding arena. And it got worse. He was nappy at all times but particularly out hacking. One day he spooked and returned to the yard down the road at a fast canter – then reared up and landed on a car bonnet. I wasn't there at the time but it certainly frightened me. I called the previous owner. She told me it was my problem and that I had caused it. I thought about legal redress but couldn't face yet more hassle and decided to put it down to experience and sell him on.

I sold him to a capable rider for a third of the price I had paid. She knew about his nappiness because I told her. She saw the video and liked it too. The relief I felt as he walked onto her trailer and the ramp closed behind him was immense. But the impact on me was far reaching. The horse robbed me of confidence in horses. The previous owner robbed me of confidence in horsey people, especially those selling horses.

I kept in touch with J's new owner. She worked with him for a couple of years but said he would never make a competition horse (after a few scarey moments at shows) and she sold him on to a rider without ambitions this way.

After J I stuck like a limpet to Shantie. He was the only horse I could trust for a long time. Gradually I recovered my confidence and started to look for another horse. Shantie was getting older and I knew his limbs weren't up to the stresses of dressage.

I must have viewed over seventy horses over a period of several years. I know I lost count. It became an obsession with me. The feeling of excitement and anxiety as the Horse & Hound dropped through my letterbox was unbelievable. I drove miles viewing horses. The feeling of excitement and anxiety as we got closer to each destination - this could be the one. Several of them probably could have been the one, but I didn't trust myself to make decisions like this any more. When the crunch came I couldn't do it. It mattered too much. I had to get it right. But I didn't know how to!

Equally, the sort of horse that I wanted was what everyone wanted; and it would be unlikely to be for sale. It must be responsive and forwards, but safe. Good paces but comfy to sit to. 100% in all circumstances – stable, field, hacking. About 16hh. A gelding.

Shantie developed a shoulder lameness when he reached 19 years old and I decided, with the advice of the vet, to retire him. He said the money I would spend on investigations (for he was too old for insurance to cover him) would be better spent on a new younger horse. This gave me a renewed impetus. I decided to narrow the search. I had visited Portugal and enjoyed riding the Lusitano horses there. I decided to only look at horses of Iberian origin.

Soon after, I found Relampago (Eric to his friends) - a 15.3hh Grey 6 year old pure bred Lusitano gelding. The minute I saw his face looking over the stable door I knew I wanted him. He wasn't perfect in the stable. He seemed anxious. He wasn't perfect to ride. He was unbalanced and unsteady in the contact. But none of this seemed to matter. I liked him and I wanted to work with him. Imagine the surprise of my partner when I returned home..."Hi, was he the one". "Yes". "Sorry I didn't hear that". "Yes I'm going to have him". "Are you sure?" "No, but I want him."

I nearly blew it after that though as the old doubts returned when the owner at first refused to give me a warranty. After an anxious weekend of soul searching I spoke to the owner again, shared my past experiences, and he shared his and suddenly it was obvious. I wanted to buy the horse and give him a home for life. The owner wanted the same thing! It was OK. We were all OK.

Eric has filled all my expectations and more. As a friend commented, "he was born about the time you first started to search for another horse – he was born for you".

My conclusion? Buying a horse is an emotional purchase not a logical one. If it feels right do your homework and check out the logic. If that doesn't work forget it! If the logic works, but it doesn't feel right, walk away. You'll know inside if he's the one.

> *What tales can you tell about buying horses? What advice would you give to others?*

Building a strong support network

> *"Understand and accept that things may take a little longer to achieve. Make sure that your partner/family are on your side in terms of support and background help with domestic chores, etc. which will enable you to fit in the required amount of training, fittening work, etc. Learn to prioritise."* Hilda Rodger (35)

The truth is that horses can get you down. You're going to need the best support network you can get especially if you work too!

It helps to think about who has a stake in your riding ambitions. These are people who are affected by, or who unfluence, your riding ambitions. Make a list. Examples could include your partner, coach, friends, boss, livery yard owner, grooms, feed/hay suppliers, vet, farrier, organisations eg British Dressage, British Riding Clubs.

Then go through each sequentially and ask "What do I need from them?" and "What do they need from me?" Put yourself in their shoes. It may help to go and talk to each of them about this. How is what you receive and give different to what is needed? What can you do about it?

Choosing a trainer
The less you know the more you need someone with lots of integrity if you are to fulfil all your potential. Unfortunately, often when we first try something we do not know our aspirations, and bad habits developed early on can have a big knock on impact.

We are all trainers and students, whether we are aware of this or not. We are all trainers because we influence those we come into contact with. Just because we don't earn our living as a trainer we still have responsibilities to others. We are all students because there is always more to learn. Effective individuals know this and make this the business of their life - continuously learning and sharing.

In the UK good training can be very expensive. This is due in part to the huge overheads in operating a riding establishment. In February 2006 a little research on the net revealed prices for a 40-45 minute private lesson varying from £25 upwards. At Huntley School of Equitation (a BHS training establishment) the price of a one hour private lesson varied from £20 for a lesson with a BHS Trainee to £43 for a FBHS. Celebrity trainers can charge double this figure!

I want to encourage you to see your training as a long term investment in yourself. The resources required for training, time and money, are scarce for the majority of working riders. This means that we need to choose how to spend our training budget wisely to obtain the best return on our investment.

After each investment ask yourself some questions. Was it worth it? How else could I have spent my time and money? Could I have achieved more by investing my hard earned cash/free time elsewhere?

Personally speaking, I would train someone who really wants to learn for free, for the rewards of training such a person are worth far more than money to me. On the other hand I would not accept a king's ransom to teach someone who has no wish to understand and work towards sustainable results for the long term. Having said this, I guess trainers make different choices when their livelihood depends on it.

There is a chemistry that comes from a strong training partnership. The relationship is symbiotic, not parasitic. Both share the same goals and ways of working. Both feed on each other. Both bring out the best in each other. They recognise that each is less without the other. Both are in it for the long term. The foundations of this are honesty, open mindedness, a desire to continuously learn and improve, two way communication and feedback.

Do you remember school? What affected your choice of subjects?

If you are like me you chose subjects partly because you liked the teacher and wanted to continue learning from them. What made you want to do that? For me it was because they were:

- Enthusiastic
- Made the subject interesting
- Fair and consistent
- Quick to notice – to correct and to reward
- Saw my success as their success
- Gave their all.

It is the same for a riding teacher!

Things to pay attention to:
- How they make you feel
- Their words – do they make sense?
- Ability to understand you and your horse as individuals
- Their focus – their attention should be entirely on you in a private lesson
- Their behaviour. Is it aligned with their words?
- Integrity
- Ability to communicate and explain
- Encouragement of 2-way communication and questions
- Ability to receive feedback
- They are committed to learning and improving themselves.

Suggested indicators of a good trainer:
- Loyal clients
- Record of improving a broad range of clients
- Sustained horses (horses working into old age)
- Record of improving a broad range of horses.

Things to ignore:
- Price (but watch your budget)
- Qualifications
- Fame
- Competition success
- Level of judge listing
- How well they ride your horse.

Remember that no-one will care as much about your training as you. Eventually you will reach a point where you realise this and the relationship between you and your teacher will have to change. From being a teacher and facilitator, imparting knowledge and facilitating your development of feel, to being a mentor. A sounding board. You set the agenda and they follow. Some will not like this change in the "balance of power".

A good coach will be your trampoline, helping you to achieve greater heights but catching you when you fall. It's still possible to train without one. It's just more difficult. And you'll need to be even more disciplined.

Eyes on the ground are invaluable. Many trainers believe this is important. Some non-horsey people have a natural feel for the way things should look. My mum is like this. If you don't have someone like this then make judicious use of mirrors and video.

Having said that your best teacher is your horse and the very best teacher is a sensitive horse.

Teaching styles

Over the years I have observed many different trainers working with horses and riders, from the BHSAI teaching a new beginner at a local riding school, to top trainers coaching top riders. I have noticed a vast range of teaching styles:

"Instructor" – literally instructs (shouts instructions). There are a lot of these about, reflecting the military origin of rider training;

"Rider" – rides your horse through you; they can't wait to get on and demonstrate;

"Presenter" - imparts knowledge in a memorable way (tells you what to do and why to do it but could be biased towards their own proposition);

"Teacher" – imparts knowledge; checks pupil has understood; a good one will explain what and why – balanced ie "I reached this conclusion because";

"Coach" – motivates - presents the options and their assessment. Let's you choose;

"Eyes on ground" – rather like a judge; often factual input – eg "too deep!"

"Suggester" – makes suggestions eg "how would it feel if...you were to ride him up a hill"

"Facilitator" – helps the pupil by making her conscious of the learning process – "What's happening; What are you feeling; Whats going on; What may be causing that?; What could we do about it?" – imparts suggestions – "have you thought about x" – keeps up to date with latest thinking

"Specialist" – teaches a particular movement well; tells you what to do but not why or how; "there's my way or the highway".

A really good trainer is able to use each of these styles and knows when each is appropriate.

I believe that it isn't sufficient that a teacher can "do". A teacher must also be able to understand why she can "do" and be able to communicate this to help her pupil.

The current training regimes create many "instructor – riders" in my experience. The development of a cadre of riding teacher called "remedial" tells us that things don't always go to plan. I understand that the BHS is aiming to ameliorate this situation with the introduction of coaching certificates.

Training Sessions
There should be a clear structure for each session including:
Planning - What do you want to work on and why? Setting goals. Agreeing the contract – the purpose of the lesson; ways of working together. What do you want to have achieved at the end of this session? Longer term? How will you know this lesson has been successful?
Understanding – The history "Tell me about you and your horse. Problems and successes".
Diagnosis – understanding how the problems manifest themselves and likely causes.
Experimentation – trying out different ideas for improvement.
Conclusion – what went well; what could be done differently (on both sides); what to work on.

You can always learn something. Even from a bad teacher.
A good teacher will see what the horse needs to work on that day AND what the rider needs to work on. The rider will always limit the horse, so the rider needs to be focussed on first. Correct the rider and you will have some chance of correcting the horse. Class lessons limit the ability to correct the horse. And often impose a set order of things. This is the same in exercise classes.

Consider a group Pilates lesson. The problem with a group is that there will be different abilities and even in a class of identical abilities we will all feel differently on the day. Some will want to go more quickly, others slowly, some will need to focus on upper body, others lower etc. Once the pupil starts to feel this the class lessons can be very frustrating and unhelpful unless operated by a trainer happy with open order. At this stage the pupil is leader and the teacher "assists" – some teachers will not like to give up their position as leader.

Sometimes teachers we have worked with for a long time develop what might be called "teacher blindness". A teacher suffering from such has become bored and in a rut. They fail to see or fail to correct faults and just accept them as part of you. If you think your teacher is suffering it is time to get a new fresh perspective.

I have been on the receiving end of some very innovative training sessions. John Micklem has a unique way of helping riders to learn about feel. On a circle, John will approach the horse, moving with the horses rhythm and tempo, and take up the reins in between the riders' hands and the horse's mouth (arm over the horses neck). This allows John to give the horse the contact required and to assess the quality of the rider's contact. As John is so tall he can do this with any height of horse in all three paces (including a 17hh Irish Draught cross thoroughbred in canter!).

By doing this John achieves two improvements. First, he regains the softness in the horse on behalf of the rider, and second, he can give the rider direct feedback on her quality of contact on behalf of her horse. John growling "get off my left hand" serves as a pertinent reminder to riders that the horse can't speak, but that we need to learn to understand his response.

Sophie Volet, a French trainer I am currently working with, often rides one of her horses with me. That way she can demonstrate the exercises we are using and she can give me feedback from lots of different points of view. For example, from behind if she follows me and from various places in the arena. I find this very useful.

I asked my survey respondents (see list in appendix) what advice they would give to an owner-rider with a full-time non-equestrian job aiming to improve her riding and her horse? Here are some of the answers:

"Read and study as much as you can but watch other trainers and riders at work. That is the best way to learn. Work out a plan of what you are able to do and aim for small goals, don't beat yourself up about what you have not got time to do. Most people spend far too little time thinking

*about how to ride, watching those who ride well, looking at videos of
people riding well or reading books about it. You can make up for the
small amount of time spent in the saddle and the fact that you probably
only ride one horse in this way. So many people never watch anyone else
or try and learn except for perhaps a lesson every week or two and then
they expect to ride like Carl (Hester) and get cross with their horses
when it doesn't happen."*

*****

*"Be realistic about yourself, your horse and your ambitions; realism
doesn't need to be limiting but there is a major difference in thought
and execution between dreams and goals*
*Learn to ride properly – develop a good, secure, balanced and correct
position before you have a horse of your own, of any level or ability.*
*Horses are 'trained' every time they are ridden; make sure you do it in a
positive, correct manner*
*Find a good trainer, who is also a good rider and trainer of horses, and
with whose philosophy you are in sympathy, and stick with them through
thick and thin.*
*Get yourself sufficiently fit to actually ride your horse instead of just
sitting on top of it*
*Try to ride, or have your horse ridden, regularly – so early mornings, late
nights, whatever it takes. If in full-time occupation, and with a family,
which so many riders are, and if finances allow, keep the horse in livery
with the trainer*
*Go to as many seminars, conferences, clinics and so on as you can and
pick from them the information that you find useful and can apply within
your own training; discuss, argue, read, watch, do"*

*****

*"Watch and read as much as you can. Be systematic in your approach
and do not rush. You do not have to prove anything to anybody - it is a
hobby and is about building a partnership with your horse. You do not
need a quick fix. Try and have regular lessons with a trainer you agree
with and respect. We all need eyes on the ground as we get in to bad
habits.*

*Understand and accept that things may take a little longer to achieve.
Make sure that your partner/family are on your side in terms of support*

and background help with domestic chores, etc. which will enable you to fit in the required amount of training, fittening work, etc. Learn to prioritise."

*****

"Look after your own horse. Build on strengths. Make your own mind up. Never ride with a watch. Training is about timing not about time. Develop your own style – don't copy – it's never a perfect copy!"

*****

"Above all enjoy your riding and treat your horse humanely, and realise that extraordinary things are possible when there is a special relationship with a horse. Ask yourself which aspects of your work with horses give you the greatest enjoyment and satisfaction then in conjunction with a coach (and an assessment by that coach if they are new to you) decide on small action steps which will help you improve in these areas and fit in with a progressive training programme."

*****

"Go and watch others. Sit in with a judge. Ride a schoolmaster. Never be afraid to ask questions. Remember that it is easy to become fixated on one thing and to forget the over picture eg. why is my shoulder in not happening... are you in a strong balanced position with correct aids and supple seat, or are you leaning in looking at the bend and in doing so restricting with your hand? Become self aware. Video yourself, cringe but look how it highlights good points and areas for improvement"

*****

"Make sure you find time to tell your horse you love him. Don't just tack up and ride then leave. After a ride, rub him down, give him a little scratch on the withers, bury your cheek in his neck and whisper to him how grateful you are that he let's you be part of his world. Mean what you say!"

Assessment and Feedback

I feel that a crucial element of improvement is continuous assessment of performance. We have seen that things can look very different depending where you stand – so this implies that for well rounded performance we need to capture a range of opinions on our progress.

Who helps you to assess your riding performance?
Do you feel satisfied with the amount and quality of feedback you
receive? If not, why not?

In my business work, career development was structured around an
annual appraisal process. This was punctuated by two key appraisals
every six months with the consultant's staff manager. One of these
appraisals was primarily backwards looking and was about assessing
performance. The other was primarily forwards looking and focussing
more on goal setting and action planning. Between these key events
consulting staff received regular feedback in the form of project
appraisals with project managers (specific to a piece of work and usually
in consultation with clients).

For the annual performance assessment, consultants also gathered 360
degree feedback. This utilised a basic feedback form highlighting 3 key
strengths and development opportunities. This form was sent to a
sample of individuals the consultant had worked with. These included
those working for the consultant, as well as senior staff, to provide a
rounded view. Those providing feedback were encouraged to give
specific and balanced feedback. Statements of behaviour patterns were
to be supported by examples. The consultant and the appraiser
completed various sections of the form separately and independently
before the appraisal meeting. The consultant also provided an "upward
review" for the staff manager (strengths and development
opportunities). The contents of the form were discussed and
irregularities addressed in the appraisal meeting. The aim of the process
was to achieve a consensus on recent performance and a way forward.

I found this structured and rigorous approach to performance
assessment to be very useful indeed. It is something that I feel is
lacking in riding performance assessment. In general, the rider receives
very little of what I call balanced feedback. And hardly any written
feedback at all. Dressage competitors are privileged to receive written
feedback on their test performance. I wonder how many see it that
way?

It is easy for me to draw comparisons between my project appraisals at work and the test assessment of a dressage judge. However, what seems to be missing is how these individual test assessments fit within an overall performance improvement regime.

Another potential problem is that the dressage test sheets are often seen as primarily "horse" assessments. There is only one explicit rider mark on the sheet and one rarely sees the full range of this mark being used! It is worth noting that at the equivalent of our British Dressage Elementary tests, in France the collective mark for the rider has a coefficient of 4!

Talent spotting competitions exist for our younger riders and these appear to be well organised and supported. But what about we older riders? Indeed, for the non-competing rider there doesn't appear to be any structured feedback scheme at all.

The British Horse Society (BHS (40)) and Association of British Riding Schools (ABRS) provide a regime of examinations. I have studied for and taken BHS stage examinations. These are assessments at a point in time and are unidirectional (no discussion involved). They do not provide the kind of opportunity that an annual or six monthly appraisal provided in my work.

I think that if we want this then the impetus will have to come from riders. Get yourself a file. Keep all your dressage test sheets. Afterwards, perhaps with your coach, note down the issues arising and agree an action plan to address them. Once or twice a year arrange a dismounted meeting with your coach (or an independent person) and work through an appraisal. Gather 360 feedback in advance of this meeting. If you don't want to do this actively then make believe you are them. What would your horse, other horses you ride, your friends, your trainers say about you. Be brutally honest.

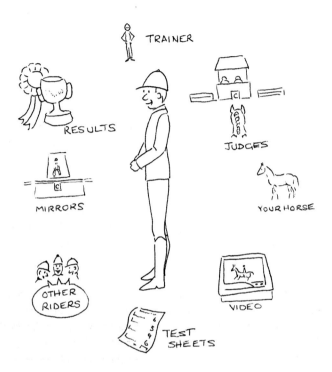

Figure 32 360 Feedback

Set yourself up to three SMART goals (Specific, Measurable, Achievable, Realistic, Time frame) for the year ahead;
Try to capture your longer term vision as well eg to be on the Olympic Team; to be the best rider I can be; to enjoy my relationship with my horse.

Use these and your development opportunities to work out how to address the gaps and to prioritise;
Think through your SWOT (Strengths, Weaknesses, Opportunities, Threats).

For example:
Strengths – body shape, motivation
Weaknesses – tension, back pain
Opportunities – Pilates lessons, riding other horses
Threats – insufficient time

You will need to make best use of the resources you have - Time, Money, Health, Knowledge – and your connections. Remember, if you fail to plan you plan to fail.

Prioritisation
If you only have a certain amount of "horse time" in a day manage it well to maximise the time you spend training your horse. I know a lot of people who spend most of their time caring for their horse and pay others to ride "because they don't have the time". This can kick off a vicious cycle that can be difficult to break out of!

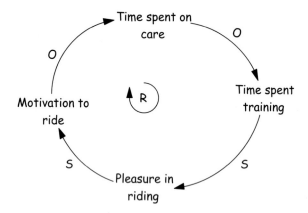

Figure 33 A Vicious Spiral

As we spend more time on care, we have less time for training. A poorly trained horse is less of a pleasure to ride and we may decide not to ride so much. This gives us more time to spend on care and the cycle persists.

When I was working in my previous career, a typical 24 hours for me used to involve

8 hours: sleeping
4 hours: travelling to and from work
8 hours: (minimum) working
2 hours: eating, cooking, shopping, household tasks
2 hours: horses.

If we have only 2 hours a day to spend on our horses then we must try to find ways of maximising the amount of that time we use for training. Ideas for this can include:

- Finding a yard nearby.
- Getting stable work done for you. If you prefer to care for your horses yourself, or can't afford to pay for care, then you could save time on mucking out by using rubber mats and a sprinkling of shavings. Mucking out takes 5 minutes this way and your muck-heap will be smaller and better quality.
- Save time watering by fitting auto-drinkers. These are great news for bad backs too.
- Save time on grooming and rug changing by using good breathable multipurpose outdoor rugs with "polishing" linings. Neck covers are invaluable for muddy winter paddocks.
- Avoid the urine smell so common in rubber matted stables (and all over your horses coat!) by teaching your horse to go for a pee outside. It didn't take mine long to understand. They come in at 5pm. At 10 pm they are let out or walked out for a pee. Again at 8am the next morning. The signal to pee is a low pitched whistle. A pee at the right time gets a "good boy" and a caress. Even cleaner stables and horses. NB This requires consistency!
- Save time tack cleaning by minimising tack (eg no noseband) and using synthetic tack.
- Feed hay on the floor. It's more natural for the horse and saves time filling and hanging nets.
- Maybe you prefer mucking out, grooming and tack cleaning to riding. If so, it's not a problem – come and do mine for me too! But

be aware and accept that your rate of progress with your riding will be slower.

- Why not use your non-horse time to work on your riding too? Use your commuting time to read those training books; think about your balance and posture; plan your next training session or analyse your last one.

- At work, think about your posture. Make better use of your breaks at work - use them to stretch and practice Pilates. Test the boundaries of what could be possible on the flexible working front eg working part-time or working more from home. There is no doubt that some jobs can negatively impact your riding in more ways than just time. Sitting at a computer all day, lots of stress and tight deadlines can all create mental and physical tension which are the great enemy of the rider. You have to decide what's more important to you. I tried working part-time and had a couple of career breaks to really focus on horses but what work did to my head and body when I was there was difficult to overcome on my horse.

My survey respondents had the following advice for a working owner rider:

"Find the right horse to suit your lifestyle and find an easy way to keep him. Enjoy your riding. Make time. Love your horse."

"Regular sessions for the horse ridden by her chosen trainer to help take his education forward faster than she can achieve."

"Ride as much as possible but it should always be a pleasure, don't let it dominate your life to the point of becoming frustrated with lack of time, and possibly involve a good trainer to help school and exercise the horse for them. Try to have a weekly lesson."

"Try and spend as much time riding as possible to keep up the fitness of horse & rider or alternatively get a sharer of the same ability as yourself"

Things to remember
Be focussed and plan.
Choose a horse you like and who you enjoy working with.
Choose a coach you like, who is committed to you and your horse's long term progress and who you enjoy working with.
Seek feedback and be honest with yourself.
Prioritise.

11 Thoughts on Equipment

"Make sure you find time to tell your horse you love him. Don't just tack up and ride then leave. After a ride, rub him down, give him a little scratch on the withers, bury your cheek in his neck and whisper to him how grateful you are that he let's you be part of his world. Mean what you say!" Mal Phillips (33)

Over the last ten years or so there has been an explosion in the quantity and quality of equipment for horse and rider. How much of this is fashion and marketing led I leave you to decide. However, it does leave we poor horse people with choices to make. For some the choice can be bewildering and, particularly for our horses, we can give away our power (and money) to some unworthy individuals if we are not careful.

The watchwords for me with all equipment are function (it can fulfil it's purpose), comfort (it fits) and value (for money).

Horse equipment
On most occasions we will ride our horse in a saddle and bridle. The bridle consists of a bit(s), headpiece, noseband and reins. The saddle has various permutations and auxiliary equipment (eg girths, stirrup leathers, numnahs, pads etc).

Let's consider the bridle first.

Bits
The bit must be comfy for the horse. It needs to be the right width and a suitable thickness. But remember, the bit is only as light as the hands on the other end of it. Some individuals are brutal with a snaffle, believing that it is a soft bit. A soft rubber mullen mouth or Nathe snaffle is a very soft bit. A thin jointed stainless steel snaffle can be a weapon of destruction. Note the use of the word "can". The bit that fits and is correctly adjusted can only become an instrument of torture in uncaring hands.

Usually we only consider the effect of the bit on the horse, but what about the way it affects the rider? An important aspect of the bit is the way it affects the psychology of the rider. In my experience curb bits encourage quieter hands. I always remember the first time my coach had me ride her horse with only the curb part of a double bridle. It was amazing the effect this had on me. I was so conscious of my hands and keeping them soft and quiet and forwards thinking.

Loose ring, jointed snaffle bits tend not to encourage quiet mouths in mouthy horses. The joint allows more room for the tongue so may be more comfy but young horses will tend to play with anything that moves...and in time that can become a habit. Other jointed snaffle exponents explain that the joint means that each side of the bit can be used independently. First of all, I don't believe that this is the case; the two sides are, after all, attached. Secondly, I believe that the hand receives. The body does the steering and speed adjustment. So why would we do different things with each side of the bit?

Some authors are adamantly against jointed snaffle bits. They "demonstrate" the action of the snaffle by encouraging riders to wrap one around their arm and pull on the reins (ouch!). This makes no sense to me. Firstly, the conformation of the human arm is nothing like a horse's mouth. Secondly, no bit should be pulled on like this whether in a horse's mouth or around a human's arm.

Heather Moffett (11) recommends a mullen mouth rubber covered Pelham with two reins. I have used this bit on my Lusitano horse who was very "mouthy" and have found the stillness, stability and security it engenders has allowed him to build confidence and quietly accept the bit. It is possible to soften the effect with an elastic curb chain or rubber covers. For the rider, the two reins give more options for finer control. I can ride on the snaffle rein alone, or the curb alone, or both reins. It is an opportunity for some good practice before moving on to a double bridle. Again, dealing with two reins helps to ensure attention to the hands. Of course, if you compete in dressage this is not an option you can consider.

For horses that do not like a curb try a mullen mouth D ring snaffle for a similar effect. One friend of mine uses an elastic curb chain with this to provide even greater security without the leverage of the curb action.

Bits are available in many different materials including stainless steel, plastic, rubber, vulcanite, aurigan, cyprium and sweet iron to name just a few. The newer metal mixtures are said to encourage the horse to accept and mouth the bit.

My trainer believes that the best bit is a simple one. She prefers a loose ring snaffle bit with a single joint and a wide mouthpiece with some weight to it. She does not like light bits with narrow mouthpieces. For young horses she prefers to use a double jointed training bit with a lozenge. She does not like the feel of the lighter plastic bits for young horses. If she wants to soften the effect of a metal bit she wraps it in leather.

Some classicists say that the only acceptable bits are the snaffle and the double bridle. But they often fail to explain why. Perhaps this is just the way it has always been done. Whilst I aim to follow classical principles I also have an open funnel to new thinking and making my own mind up about what makes sense and what doesn't. I suggest you do too.

Klaus Ferdinand Hempfling explains the classical progression of bitting in his book "Dancing with Horses" (19). He starts a young horse with 2 pairs of reins attached to the cavesson and a bridoon bit. Then a curb is added and the reins are attached to the bridoon and curb. Eventually he progresses to a curb bit with a single pair of reins. He says "a horse bitted in this way has reached the peak of his craft".

There are some very expensive bits available nowadays. But I ask you, do our horses go any better in them? The key is comfort and fit. I see no relationship between price and way of going. At the end of the day the biggest difference is the hand on the other end of the rein.

Do we need to use a bit at all?

I asked William Micklem this question. Here are his thoughts –

"It's a good question....do we need to use something to control the direction and speed? Yes, otherwise it gets pretty exciting when there are groups of horses despite the possibility of riding without a bridle/bit. What are the alternatives? Tongue attachments..the oldest type of control mechanism, still used in Western riding, but not pleasant to see a severed tongue or partially severed tongue. Bitless bridles mainly work on pressure round the jaw which can be extremely uncomfortable, especially as the upper jaw is so much wider than the lower jaw. Some of the USA ones are sheer cruelty...although there are more mild forms which are great in a controlled and quiet environment but in practise often prove dangerous for other riders and spectators.

I always want to see how a horse goes without a bit before deciding on the next step and I know that many horses are transformed in both behaviour and way of going without the bit that was uncomfortable to them. Most of these horses need one or more of the following: attention to the teeth, a change of noseband, a period of time without a bit, a period of training to get them to use their backs, time for cracks and tissue damage to heal up, a more allowing hand.....but in my experience at the end of the day most will be more comfortable in a bit than with a bitless bridle. The majority of horses appreciate less pressure on the tongue...hence two of the uses of my Micklem Multibridle...not available at the moment but soon I hope..."

Nosebands
Why use a noseband?
Possible answers could be
1. Because I have to when I compete so the horse will be familiar;
2. For aesthetic reasons – it makes his head look better balanced;
3. To keep his mouth shut;
4. To encourage him to have a quiet mouth;
5. Because everyone else does;
6. Never really thought about it, it came with the bridle!

Let's consider each response in turn.

1. OK – an acceptable reason. As long as it's correctly adjusted, comfy for the horse and not tight.
2. Seems reasonable for showing, but at home, why bother with all the extra cleaning?
3. The horse is opening his mouth for a reason. We need to discover the root cause and fix that. If not we will always need to use a strong noseband. And less freedom means either more attempts by the horse to get free, or a brow beaten horse. Some riders have the mindset that their horse will look to avoid work, and perhaps some do. However, I prefer to take a more positive view.
4. Setting a boundary for a young horse is fine. Many classical trainers recommend a correctly adjusted drop noseband as the best choice at this point.
5. You need to be clear why *you* do it. Who gives a damn about everyone else.
6. Time to start thinking.

I only use a loose cavesson for cosmetic reasons, however I generally don't use one as it means extra cleaning and less time for riding. It also means that you don't need to spend lots of money on fancy "elevator" style bridles as without a noseband there are no pressure points at the poll.

I dislike any noseband designed to restrict the horse. If the horse opens his mouth it is a sign of other problems and we need to trace the root causes and fix those rather than try to "hide the symptom". I also think that a horse who is not allowed to express himself in his mouth develops problems in other parts of his body.

If I was the FEI I would not allow nosebands in dressage competitions for this reason. Nothing beautiful can be forced or restricted.

Other parts of the bridle must fit. I often see brow bands which are too tight or too loose. My Lusitano is a cob size overall but needs a full size brow-band as he is broad across the forehead. Don't buy a complete bridle and expect that all parts of it will fit. Some horses are not off the peg like this.

Podhajsky's Complete training (14) shows photos from the Spanish Riding School of horses with bridles without a throat lash. Also KFH doesn't see any use for a throat lash and cuts them off. He says they have no purpose. I am inclined to agree but before doing the deed I decided to monitor my use of the throat lash. I discovered that I use the throat lash to secure my reins when tacking up and when lunging before riding. I concluded that my throat lash did have a use and haven't cut mine off!

What items of tack do you have which are excess to requirements?

Saddles
In my experience saddles can be a major bugbear for a less experienced owner. And yet a good saddle makes a big difference.

On my search for a new horse I came across some truly awful saddles. Some horses were presented almost crippled in "a friends saddle I have borrowed". For this reason, when trying a horse for sale, it is worth checking out the tack being used. Don't reject a good horse due to poor-fitting tack.

I learnt about saddles by making mistakes. When I bought Shantie he came with all his tack. Great, I thought, therefore it's bound to fit. I had a saddler to check the saddle anyway and she adjusted the flock behind the shoulders. A combination of additional pressure due to hard packed flock and bad riding led to some rather nasty saddle sores. Shantie still has the white hair scar patches to prove it.

I had the Balance people out to help. They showed me how to take wither patterns to monitor my horse's shape. I rode bareback on a polypad for many years after that. It gave me a different perspective on saddles and why I needed one and therefore what was important to me about it.

People who say that bareback riding is cruel to the horse have never ridden bareback. It makes you very aware of your balance, and being truly let down and relaxed. However, you need a comfy backed horse that you can trust. You learn that a lot of the rider's weight is supported on the thighs, and not on the seat bones as is commonly thought.

I only used a saddle for road hacking and jumping. I had an Albion GP that I bought new from a reputable saddler (fitted by him). Two years later another reputable saddler said it didn't fit and it was causing my back problems. She fitted a wider GP with a prolite pad. She explained her philosophy, that the saddle needed to be wider than the horse, as well as needing padding (socks) like a good pair of walking boots. It worked for me but how much of this was down to an improvement in my balance and how much to the saddle is another question entirely.

Which leads me to another important finding. Good saddles don't make up for unbalanced riding. Changing the saddle is a quick fix that will always fail in the long term if the rider is not sufficiently balanced and stable in the saddle. A good seat requires work, however, you can't buy a good seat.

What is a good saddle?
I think that a good saddle fits you and the horse and does not block either in any way. It is conspicuous by its absence.

The choice is bewildering. Saddles differ in many ways:
- Different purposes – dressage, GP, jumping, endurance, Trec
- Different materials – leather, suede, synthetic
- Different panel stuffing – flock, gel, air, reactorpanel
- Different trees – wood, synthetic, sprung, adjustable, western, none (treeless)
- Different girthing systems – long tabs, short tabs.

It is difficult to work out what is a difference between features for marketing's sake and those which are really useful.

I tried five saddlers when I first bought my Lusitano horse. None of them had a saddle that would fit him in stock. All of them wanted to convince me to order a made to measure new saddle. I resisted this, as a saddle belonging to the owner of the yard did fit Eric and I very well. It was a showing (working hunter) saddle so I ordered one from the supplier. "You send a template and he makes one to measure".

Do you know I received and returned five saddles, none of which fitted! The last of these to arrive still didn't fit. The yard owner said "if we use a thick numnah and a prolite wither pad etc etc it should just about fit". I repeat, this was a brand new made to measure saddle. At the time I wasn't in a fit state to make decisions about anything due to my nervous breakdown so I gave up trying and took my horse to France without a saddle.

For the horse the shape of the tree and the shape and bearing surface of the panels really matters. Horses, like humans, come in different shapes and sizes. Eric is flat through the back longitudinally (front to back) and not very wide latitudinally (side to side). Shantie is more concave longitudinally but broader laterally. The same saddle tree is unlikely to fit both.

Saddles also differ in terms of the amount of padding in the panels beneath the rider's seat. I prefer a saddle that gives a close contact feel (ie less distance from the rider's seat to the horse's back). The Passier Grand Gilbert dressage saddle is a good example of the seating arrangement I prefer.

We riders also have different conformation. See Charles Harris' "Fundamentals of Riding" (22) for a thorough exposition of the difference between the male and female conformation. Some riders prefer a deeper seat with huge knee rolls. Personally, I prefer a more open, flatter, seat with little knee roll. Some friends prefer a lot of padding on the seat. Personally, I prefer as little as possible; the closer I can sit to the horse the better. Klaus Ferdinand Hempfling (19) recommends Iberian saddles but they all look like they have masses of padding in the panels.

Girthing arrangements make a difference to saddle fitting too. Better girthing means less movement of the saddle (all things equal). The relative positioning of the horse's centre of gravity and the girth groove affects the requirement for the positioning of the girth tabs. A horse with a girth groove well in front of the centre of gravity may need a point strap. Equally, a horse with conformation the other way around may benefit from a cantilever arrangement. A three point girthing system can give better stability than only two central girthing points. The girth itself also needs to be comfy. I really like the Wintec Elastic girths. They are strong but with some elasticity and easy to care for.

Leathers can make a big difference. I find that I prefer single thickness dressage leathers. The key to it all is comfort. If you're not comfy you won't relax and if your horse isn't comfy either, because you aren't, or the saddle doesn't suit his contours, then he won't relax.

Numnahs and girths
A well fitting saddle shouldn't need a numnah but I use one to keep the saddle clean. I like one that is clearly designed to fit my horse, following his contours and with tabs in the right places. A local disciple of Portuguese riding uses leather numnahs under his saddles. This way the underside of his saddle is saved but he cleans the numnah as he would the rest of his leather tack. A truly inconspicuous numnah.

Equestrian consultant, Hilda Rodger (35), gives the following advice about numnahs and girths:

You clearly recommend riders use a numnah or pad. Why?
"They are more comfortable for the horse, because (i) they help to avoid pressure points from rider crookedness (ii) they are warmer than cold leather (iii) they absorb sweat."

Why do you recommend the Mattes numnahs?
"They are beautifully cut to 'sculpt' round the saddle; they never move; the small quilting means the stuffing never moves either; they outlast any other brand and just wash and wash without losing their shape and firmness."

Are there any types of numnahs/pads to be avoided?
"(i) foam lined (ii) large quilting with cheap lining which moves (iii)heavy gel pads which are supposed to absorb shock but actually just add weight and 'sit' on the withers and spine (iv) most cheap numnahs because the girth tabs are in the wrong place and cause all sorts of pressure point problems which usually go undiagnosed – something else is always blamed – i.e. injury/saddle/rider."

What are the characteristics of a good numnah?
"(i) It does not move (ii) it is made of natural materials which absorb sweat and do not cause skin irritation (iii) it is big enough for the saddle (iv) it is machine washable (v) it holds shape after many washes (vi) it is cut 'on the bias' to fit up into the gullet and cause no pressure on spine and withers (vii) it has girth tabs which lie with, rather than against, the angle of the shoulder blade."

Thinking about pads again! Should I take it based on your recommendations that Polypads and Prolites/ gel pads/ riser pads are "out"?

"I'm not against Polypads. They are well designed and well made. In fact, I stock and sell the Polypad Pet Beds, which are simply canine versions and sizes of the equine pads. They suit some horses and some saddles very well indeed. In fact, BALANCE originally recommended Polypads as the 'filler' for muscle wastage, until they developed their own numnah and pad system. I was a guinea pig at one of the first BALANCE demos and the demonstrator saddles were used with Polypads in those days. They don't suit every horse or every saddle though and can sometimes 'scoot out the back' or, on a wide horse with a petite rider, make the rider feel like there is too much pad between them and the horse."

(Author's note: I do use polypads myself. They are easy to use, don't move and can be reversed for less washing.)

"Prolite Pads are fine too for many horses and the BALANCE system nowadays incorporates their own design of Prolite pads.

I am, however, totally against gel pads for two reasons: (i) their weight, and (ii) because they lie on the withers and spine.

I also do NOT like riser pads – I can see no justification for them – if you need to use a riser pad, then what you REALLY need is to (i) get to the bottom of why you 'need' it – i.e. solve the horse's physiological problem and don't mask it and (ii) you need to replace your saddle."

Do you subscribe to the "BALANCE" point of view that saddles should be fitted wider (like a pair of hiking boots) and then padded out (like good walking socks) or do you believe in a well fitted saddle with a numnah for other reasons?

Your interpretation of the BALANCE approach is not quite accurate. The fitting wide and padding out is an <u>interim measure</u> to allow wasted muscles to build up again. Thereafter, the amount of padding is simply what is required for the horse's comfort.

I was attracted to the BALANCE philosophy because it made sense to me and concurred with thoughts and ideas I'd had in my own head after many years of working with and being around horses. For instance, horses ARE more comfortable wearing a correctly fitted numnah, for all sorts of reasons. So why on earth consider that a saddle can only be 'correctly' fitted to the horse's bare back, when 9 out of 10 riders will then buy it, take it away and use a numnah underneath it???!!!"

Same for girths - ie why do you recommend particular brands on your website? What are good and bad features of girths?

"I recommend the *Stubben Trevira* girth because (i) they are made of a low friction chafeless material (ii) they allow the air to circulate (iii) they are wide so spread the pressure more evenly (iv) they are hard wearing and last a long time."

Hilda has made conscious choices of equipment. She knows what she likes and why she likes it. We should all aim for this.

Synthetic saddles are commonplace in France. I sat on a Wintec 500 dressage saddle with an adjustable front gullet in the equestrian section of our local DIY shop. I liked it. I took it home and tried it on Eric. The medium gullet it came with was not wide enough for him. I tried the wide gullet and it fitted well. I bought the saddle and a set of MW,W and XW gullets so I could adjust it myself. I have found it to be one of the best value for money saddle purchases I have ever made.

Knowing what I know now, in future I would:
1. Understand and monitor my horse's shape and condition. Ideally we want our horse in normal/good condition but not obese or a hat-rack;
2. Try different saddles in shops or friends' saddles to work out my own preferences. Ask friends to share their experiences. The internet can be a good source of info. Have a look at www.newrider.com, a website that helps riders to share experiences and tips. See also www.sustainabledressage.net (Tack & Auxilliary equipment);
3. Of the ones I like I try them in my horse's size on him – statically and dynamically. Be careful. A lot of suppliers won't take a saddle back if it appears "used". Best to try a "test" saddle (good saddlers will have these) or stick to secondhand. If there are no other choices then use a thin numnah and tights over your leathers to protect the new saddle "on trial";

4. When you've found what suits shop around for the best deal. New off the peg can be cheaper by mail-order but after-sales care may not be up to much. Also, watch out for the return conditions. They may be unachievable.

A friend of mine asked me to help her to find a suitable saddle for two very wide horses she owns. She is considering a treeless saddle so that she can use it on both horses. Here are the things I advised her to consider:

The most important thing is that the saddle fits the horse and you. Not one of you! All of you! And that it is fit for purpose. Also important is that you stick within your budget.

> *Other than fit and price what is important to you? How are you going to use your saddle?*

Do the horses have a stable weight and shape or are they changing /likely to change? Monitor the shape with a flexi-curve. If overweight then put them on a diet with a lot of dismounted work and monitor changes with the flexi-curve.

If both horses are in equilibrium but the shapes are different then you must accept that one will be less comfortable than the other in the same conventional saddle. This gives the following options:
1. With one saddle it is better to fit the wider horse and pad it up for the one that is less wide;
2. Or you must buy 2 saddles;
3. Or you get a saddle you can adjust yourself eg the Wintec. However, even these saddles are not designed for continuous adjustment. More adjustment means more wear;
4. Or you buy a treeless saddle;
5. Or you don't ride one of them in a saddle - try bareback – thus providing many of the advantages of the treeless saddles for no outlay.

Let's consider the treeless option first.
I think an entirely treeless saddle could create problems. The good so-called treeless saddles are not treeless at all. They have a front arch (gullet) that raises the saddle over the withers and ensures a fit without slipping. Slipping can be a problem on most rotund horses. Treeless saddles are relatively structure free for the rider and have more of a bareback feel, so are unlikely to suit those who prefer a saddle with a deeper seat and more of a support structure.

Treeless saddles are often made from softer leathers. For example, nubuck leather is very soft but therefore not as hardwearing. I wouldn't ride in the rain in a saddle made of this material because it is porous and will absorb moisture.

Now for mass produced wide saddles.
These tend to be cheaper, especially the synthetic ones. Thorowgood make a Griffin GPX and a Maxam Cob. However, they are not adjustable. The Wintec Wide is well made, is adjustable and has a 3 point girthing system for added stability. However, all of these are GP saddles, although straighter cut than most GP saddles (so called VSD, very slightly dressage style) to accommodate the bigger shoulders of a cob type horse.

Another thing to watch for is that a lot of wide saddles, especially older style ones, are also wide through the twist, which will affect your sitting position. This is not pleasant, especially if you have a back problem. The Wintec claims to overcome this problem.

GP vs specialised? Horses for courses!
A good GP saddle is worth its weight in gold. You can use it for flat-work, hacking and jumping. The problem with a deep seated dressage saddle with big knee rolls is that it is much less versatile. Fine if all you want to do is flatwork with long stirrup length. If you wanted to go for a gallop or pop a few fences it's possible in the Wintec 500 dressage saddle. You can put the stirrups up because there is no knee roll. But if I

planned to do this regularly I'd get myself a decent GP - maybe another Wintec.

There are many other options including Western saddles, Randonee saddles eg Zaldi Raid and Endurance saddles (sometimes like GP's but with shorter flaps and broader bearing surfaces). I am unable to comment on these as I have never tried them.

Lunge Tack and facilities
Side reins – Make sure they are long (often difficult to find them long enough) and adjustable, with evenly positioned holes on each rein. When using the side reins make sure that they are correctly adjusted; better a little too long than too short as you don't want to block the horse with the rein. We want him to seek a contact acceptable to him.

I don't agree with lunging from the bit in most circumstances. The horse's mouth is very precious and I wouldn't risk him losing confidence should an accident happen. However, I know of many others who do so successfully. For example, Ingrid and Reiner Klimke in their book "Basic Training of the Young Horse" (13) explain that they clip the lunge rein to the inside bit ring and the ring on either a drop or a cavesson noseband. This helps to prevent the bit being pulled through the horse's mouth in the absence of side reins or a bit without cheek pieces.

A lot of the cheaper synthetic lunge cavessons are badly designed. I often just use a normal headcollar and attach the rein to the ring underneath the chin. The Micklem multibridle looks like a fantastic piece of training kit for the young horse, including a dropped cavesson with rings for lunging and a single head piece (see William Micklem's book (5)).

Brushing boots all round are good practice, especially for a young or unknown horse or indeed any horse with shoes. I tend not to use brushing boots with my boys as they are not shod and so far I have not had any brushing injuries either when working or when turned out.

Gloves are absolutely essential for the trainer. A number of summers ago it was very hot and I was lunging without gloves when a neighbour put up a large parasol in their garden that had a border with my school. Shantie spooked and galloped off. The rope burns I got on my hands before I could drop the rein nearly made me faint! A very painful experience and needless to say I learnt my lesson the hard way. Always wear gloves, even when it's hot, or don't lunge.

Shoes

Pilates is done barefoot as it enables the human to feel the support points in their feet and so to improve their sense of balance. Could it be the same for the horse?

Certainly, the frog in most shod horses does not contact the ground. This means that the horse can't feel the ground so well. My horses are barefoot now and their feet are good. However, this has not always been the case. Shantie has never worn back shoes and his hind feet have always been excellent. In contrast his front feet were poor when shod.

Since removing the shoes I have had no brushing or over-reach injuries (or indeed kick injuries or injuries resulting from losing shoes in the field). My farrier bill is a fraction of what it was as I do a lot of the care myself. For more information on footcare see the Barefoot Horse internet sites in the appendix (36).

Most leisure horses do not need shoes. In fact they probably need shoes like a hole in the head. But we are afraid to change. Why? There is always a bad patch when a change is made. For a while the horse's feet will "break up" due to nail holes splitting, as well as the feet getting used to the wear. However, they will toughen up again. We can't face the problems of the transition period so we are locked into shoes for good.

Shoes have their place for horses covering many miles a day on hard and uneven abrasive ground where excessive wear would negate the benefits of being barefoot.

Rider equipment

Clothes are very personal. My priorities again are function, comfort and value.

I prefer:
- Breeches without a full seat – just good knee strapping (eg alcantara) that doesn't twist round. Fabric wise I prefer a quality cotton mix with elasticity;
- Thin gloves in summer; neoprene in winter; essential if you compete anytime, but absolutely essential in winter to avoid cold weather injuries.
- Jodphur boots and half chaps give me more leg freedom and are easier to get on and off. I find that modern boots with a contoured supportive sole are better than the old fashioned varieties.
- Well balanced dressage whip. This is one of my "props". I don't carry it always. I leave it at the side of the arena in reaching distance. When I carry it I believe my horse will canter on the aid and usually he does. I don't use the whip. It is a psychological prop for me. It works as a prop for me because he isn't whip shy and it doesn't make him tense. If he was I would de-sensitise him by carrying it always.
- Short jumping whip. Easy to carry all the time and doesn't get in the way. Can be used on your own thigh or on the numnah. The sound the whip makes is important, rather than the physical impact.
- A lightweight, well fitting, comfortable hat constructed to the current standard. I find it is amazing how many "celebrities" do not wear a hat.
- T-shirt in summer or thermal wicking tops and layers in winter.
- Riding waistcoat provides warmth where I need it but less restricting than a normal jacket.

Spurs – I believe that riders shouldn't wear spurs until they have a stable leg. You can't maintain a stable leg until you have self control and you can't have that until you have self carriage. I have witnessed riders being urged to use spurs by their trainers because their horse is lazy. It doesn't work. Spurs are for finessing leg aids, not for punishing the horse with legs the rider can't control. At one yard that recommended this approach the horses all had scars on their sides. An overactive, clinging leg can create enough damage without spurs. If you are wearing patches off your horse's coat it is time to stop and think and change your riding.

What about rider injuries? And I'm not talking about accidents and broken bones here! In the past I have had rubs under my left seat bone and blisters inside my knees. Blisters means rubbing which means movement and chafing. Why? The blisters were caused by some poorly fitting breeches and riding a rather lazy horse. Some saddles with thick stirrup leathers can cause problems so try single thickness dressage leathers.

You shouldn't need to use plasters, strapping, thick padded pants and gel/prolite seats or pads on saddles. This addresses the symptom rather than treating the cause. Usually the cause is too much rider movement due to instability. More work on position is what is required. Good riding is not about bumping and grinding. Stop clinging, gripping and pushing and simply let go and allow.

Riding surfaces
There is no doubt that a good surface builds confidence and inflicts less cumulative damage to horse's legs. What is a good surface? It is consistent, flat, cushioned, not deep, not too hard, not dusty, not flooded or frozen.

Size? A larger area encourages forwardness and you can always rope off a smaller area should you deem it necessary. A smaller area encourages balance but you will inevitably ride many more corners. A "closed" indoor arena can help with concentration but reduce forwardsness. Working outdoors can test concentration but improves forwardsness (unless the weather gets in the way).

What about an area for lunging? Over the years I have lunged in indoor and outdoor riding arenas, in lunge rings and in fields. They all have different advantages and disadvantages. Other than maintaining concentration, the main problem with using a field is the damage to the surface that lunging creates. This can be minimised by never lunging in the same place but some damage is still inevitable. A fenced circular lunge ring defines the limit of the circle and therefore acts as an 'outside aid'. However, it is difficult in a lunge ring to create straight lines or to move the circle. My preference is to lunge in an arena. In that way it is possible to use an end of the arena for control (only one open side), or to move the circle to the centre (completely open) when I have the horse's attention.

Kit affects comfort and our ability to relax, but it is not the whole solution. The wrong kit can block improvement but it certainly can't provide a constant means of acceleration towards your goals, only you can do that. Certain items of kit can help to achieve "results" more quickly but what are the side effects? Quick fixes tend not to work in the long term. There is no place for gadgets in this regime. Gadgets require great self control. They are often used to force submission rather than to encourage acceptance.

Equine companies have jumped on the marketing bandwagon. We now have potions and gadgets for every equine problem and bad habit. Just take a look in the latest horsey magazines:
He's too up – get him a calmer;
He's too slow – get him a different feed;
He won't go on the bit – get him a new bit;
These companies make their profit from our desire to do our best by our horse. But what is best for your horse? What affects his anxiety? What affects his energy? What affects his ability to go on the bit? Go on – do the thinking. It's easier to buy the product and feel that you've done your best and believe that, only you know you haven't. But you have to live with yourself – you know that deep inside. It's a cop out to avoid having to consider other options. I know this because I've done it. We all have.

Theresa Sandin shares her thoughts on tack and it's impact on dressage training on www.sustainabledressage.net. Take a look. Do you agree with her views? I don't agree with all her views. But it is wonderful to see such a full and detailed exposition of a rider's mental models.

Others who are outspoken on tack and equipment in their books are Heather Moffett (11) and Udo Burger (3).

Things to remember
Make conscious choices about the tack you use – don't simply follow the latest fashion.
Learn how to use your tack well.
Comfort is very important. If you or your horse is uncomfortable your attention is likely to be on that and you will feel less able to relax.

No relaxation, no quality riding.

---

12 The Way Forward – The Learning Rider

Don't close your heart to learning...there is always more in you.

The previous 11 chapters have been about learning new skills and attitudes. In this final chapter I help you to see how you can take these things forward, develop them further and integrate them into your life. Make this chapter the beginning of a new chapter in your own life. Even as the most knowledgeable rider on the planet we can still be a learning rider!

Figure 34 A Learning Rider

Being a "learner" has bad connotations in our society. We value achievements now rather than continuous progression and sustainability. We are constantly encouraged to want, and expect, more...now.

We may easily be able to change the way that things appear, but understanding doesn't work like that. Deeper understanding comes from continuous refinement. There is always more to learn.

In the same way, appearances are never sustainable...they are always decaying...the only sustainable thing is what is created through understanding.

Direct interventions to change appearance are never sustainable. Sustainable change comes from understanding what makes the outside appear the way it does and what makes it better or worse. Work on eliminating the things which make it worse and develop the things that make it better. In this way we fix root causes and the results are sustainable. All quick fixes ultimately fail in the long term because they do not address root causes.

What is a learning rider?
A Learning Rider...
- accepts that the only thing they can truly control is themselves...and constantly works on that basis;
- believes that blaming, frustration and anger are counter-productive and achieve nothing. She works to eliminate them from her life;
- knows that true self control comes from consistency, self forgiveness and a continuous honing of understanding;
- knows that they are the creator of their own future and sees this knowledge as empowering;
- works towards enlightenment and recognises that achievement is often in direct proportion to the impediments blocking the way;
- always starts with the end in mind.

I asked my survey respondents "what are the most important attributes of a good rider?" Here are some selected responses:

"Empathy, patience, common sense and a sense of humour."
*****
"To be generous, inquiring and demanding...all 3 are needed."
*****
"The attitude that the horse's welfare is foremost. Good physical conformation, fitness and ability to coordinate. A clear understanding of what they are trying to achieve and the knowledge of how to get there. A lack of 'achieve at all costs.'"
*****
"Feel, temperament, right physique (long legs, short back – more a model than a dumpling), fitness."
*****
"Feel. An independent seat. Good hands. Dedication to continuous improvement. Long tern commitment."
*****

The Learning Cycle
We cannot change the past but we should not ignore it. We should learn from it and apply this learning to prepare for the future. We act in the present. In this way our lives become a never-ending chain of learning (from the past), choosing (a direction for the future), acting (taking action consistent with this direction) and learning again. Planning, acting, learning...planning. As human beings we can share our learning and so we can learn from the past experiences of others too. Everyday you will learn something.

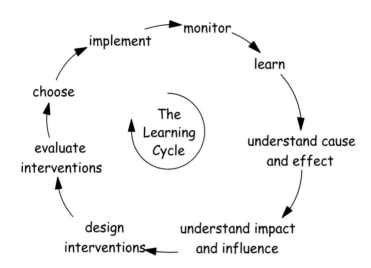

Figure 35 The Learning Cycle

You'll start to notice more if you make this learning explicit by capturing it. At the end of each day or at the start of a new one capture what you learnt in that day. Prepare to be amazed.

Active Learning
A Learning Rider strives to create a balanced mind and a balanced body.

1. A balanced mind is an emancipated mind – free from tension, free from fear and anxiety, open to continuous learning and self development, forgiving of self and others,

2. A balanced mind is an open mind. Open to new ideas, interested in everything, actively seeking new knowledge, never dismissive. Prepared to try new things. Doesn't judge too early and dismiss options.

3.   A balanced mind is a calm confident mind. A mind under control that can be used to think and to feel. A mind aware of the whole body and balance.

4.   A balanced mind is a positive mind. It is only too easy to see what's wrong. Seeing what's good and counting your blessings makes you glad. Which in turn makes you more positive and so on. There is always something good to be found in everything. So banish those negative thoughts – the only person they affect is you.

5.   A balanced mind doesn't push too hard or waste effort. If something isn't working it looks for another way. It seeks effective sustainable ways of doing things.

6.   A balanced mind trusts itself. How do we develop trust and confidence? We trust when we understand. Seek to understand.

7.   A balanced mind accepts mistakes as part of learning. Demanding perfection of ourselves – the right decisions; the perfect words; the perfect transitions etc – is destructive. Not being able to make mistakes limits our learning. Be open to experimentation and think more. "I wonder what will happen if" rather than "I must make it like this". Never blame your horse or others around you. Instead use your energy to work out what happened and what caused it. Change the things you believe will make a difference and that you can change. The most obvious (but most difficult) thing to change is always our own behaviour.

8.   A balanced mind is honest. You can fool others but you should never try to fool yourself. You can never hide from yourself.

Deep trust comes from wisdom. This is an in-depth understanding of what affects what – cause and effect – and it comes through "learning". And learning comes through thinking. Thinking is a skill in it's own right. Just as we can improve our bodily strength and suppleness so we can improve our mind.

If we see life as a stream of random events we are left feeling out of control and our only option is to react.

If we start to see patterns of events, we can start to modify our behaviour and prepare...we are no longer caught unawares but we still don't feel in control!

When we understand the structure of cause and effect behind the patterns...then we know...and we can act confidently and in control.

Improving Learning effectiveness

Our effectiveness at anything is governed by 3 factors: direction (what to work on); skills (how to work on it) and motivation (why to work on it). It is the same with learning!

Motivation is very important. Learning requires effort. Good learners are open-minded and proactive. They not only accept knowledge but go out and actively look for it. No one else can learn for you – only you. No-one else is responsible for your learning – only you. Not your school teacher, not your riding coach, ONLY YOU!!!

The learning I am talking about here is not rote learning, the cramming for exams that is then quickly forgotten. It is the learning that determines the fabric of how we live our lives, what we choose to do and how we choose to do it. This means that we don't cram at all. Instead we become discerning and selective in terms of what we choose to use and store. And we continually revisit "our accepted wisdom".

This process is best depicted as a funnel. Some people have a funnel with a tiny hole, some people have a wide funnel, some dismiss too early, some don't discard enough and waste valuable storage space and thinking time. The secret is to keep an open funnel and pro-actively seek material for it and learn to discard that which is less useful before it clogs up the system! Diverging then converging.

We need to ensure our funnel is kept open! As we get older we tend to close down our funnel. We dismiss knowledge for a variety of reasons. We are sometimes prejudiced against the source or because we are too hierarchical and dismiss knowledge from those we consider "beneath" us. My first employer taught me that this is limiting. The new graduate was seen to have as much if not more right to speak and be a source of great new knowledge.

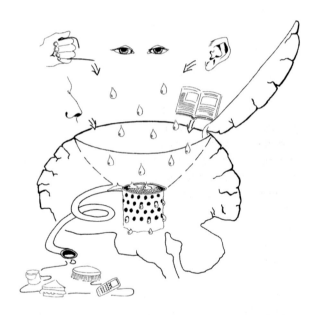

Figure 36 The Thinking Funnel

Horse riding is rather a closed minded discipline. It is very traditional, military in origin and hierarchical. Old and classical are seen to be "best" and new creative approaches seen as a "threat". There are cries of "not invented here" and "why recreate the wheel" heard everywhere! Whilst I have sympathy with not wasting effort on recreating wheels I can also see that sticking to this by the letter limits opportunities for creativity and improvement. I think that a lot of this comes from seeing the world from our own tiny perspective (like the girl with the dominos in chapter 3) and not seeing the bigger picture.

Free your mind!

Imagine you are the first human being to contemplate riding a horse. You know what you know now but you are starting again! What would you do?

Knowledge acquisition
The funnel works best when we
> (1)   Pour knowledge into it; and
> (2)   Filter that knowledge.

Where can we find knowledge? Sources of knowledge are all around us.
- Word of mouth – friends, trainers, judges.
- The written word – books, magazines, the internet, test sheets. If you can't afford books of your own try your local library. Even if they don't have the books you want they will order them in for you and membership is usually free. A recommended reading list is enclosed in the appendix.
- Pictures – photographs, drawings, paintings
- Film – video, dvd
- Spectating – at dressage competitions (tests and warm-up arena), at training sessions, at lecture-demos
- Writing - at dressage competitions

Ask yourself – what do I like and what don't I like and why? Teaming up with a friend/ group of friends can be a fun way of doing this. Find a person who you can talk to, bounce ideas off, share your thoughts and check out theirs, of good intellect but not necessarily of the same views as your own – use photos, books, videos as stimuli. "Do you agree"; "Why yes? Why not?". Relate to your own experiences.

A word of warning! I don't have a partner who is horsey. I know some of you will have! Do be careful...mine hates me to talk horse with him. He has no interest and it simply bores him and diverts him from his interests.

Active reading

At the end of each day I reach for my books. If I have been struggling with something that day I look for inspiration. If I am planning my training for the next day I seek inspiration in the same way. Each night I "train with" the best contemporary and deceased masters of equitation – What does Paul Belasik (7) say about counter canter? How about Michel Henriquet (10) and Kyra Kyrkland (18)? Does Udo Burger (3) agree? How about Nuno Oliveira (8)? I've been having problems with my seat now how can Sally Swift (12) help me with that? You get the picture?

Books are fantastic. You can carry them with you. Unlike DVD's we don't need a player to watch them. You can read selectively what you need at your convenience. They are so cheap in comparison to a lesson with the same person. I can reap the harvest of the thinking of people long since dead who have taken the trouble to pass on their most precious inheritance of all, their knowledge, not just to their families but to us all.

What of contradictions? There will always be contradictions. Life is like that. What works for one person may not work for another. This is life's rich pattern. And our challenge is to work out what works for us. Don't get too caught up in the disagreements. Think it through and make your choice about what you will try. If it doesn't work for you try to understand why. And then try again. If it still doesn't work don't push harder, try something else.

Do you have books on riding? How do you use them?

Many people indulge in what I call passive reading. This kind of reading is about passing time and what is read is forgotten almost as soon as it registers. If your time is precious, and all working riders will be in this category, you need to make your reading time count.

I find that I do two types of reading. One type is what I'd call reference reading. This is basically nugget picking. I search in the index of books for a topic I'm interested in and then just read that section. In this way I can compare and contrast many points of view. The other type of reading is what I call active reading. I'm seeking to really thoroughly understand the author's point of view. As I read I'm asking myself questions. What is the evidence for or against? Have I seen/felt this? Does it make sense? How does it fit with my mental model? Could it be true? Often I will resort to Systems Thinking to check out the logic of the argument. Well-written prose makes it easy to draw the connections. Poorly written or inconsistent prose does not!

Filtering knowledge
Never take any words as sacrosanct. Even if they are written in posh print in a book by a famous author. If an explanation is provided, check it makes sense. Seek other points of view. Use Systems Thinking to see if it makes sense theoretically.

It follows that we may miss gems of knowledge if we are put off by the packaging. Don't judge a book by its cover. It is surprising how many words of wisdom are lost with poor communication. It also follows that to get our point across we must think about our audience and the best way of reaching them.

I use Systems Thinking in a number of ways:
- To analyse and learn from a riding session that day
- To help me to understand what a book is telling me
- To help me to structure my own thoughts so that I can communicate them better.

Let me give you an example. One day I was riding Eric in the riding arena. It started off well. I felt relaxed and focussed on my relaxation. But somewhere along the way I lost it. The worse it started to feel the more demanding I became. And it felt horrible! The more I demanded, the less relaxed I became. The less relaxed the more braced and stiff I became. The more braced the less the horse could work through me and the more blocked he became. Despite this he was forwards. But the forwardsness was blocked leading to short steps and falling on the shoulders. This in turn led to a leaning on the rein. This made me feel frustrated and become even more demanding! A vicious circle if ever there was one. I tried giving the rein but it didn't work. I tried slowing the speed but it didn't work. The analysis I did in the evening helped me to understand why...

Can you draw the cause and effect diagram?
(There is an example answer below)

What does the rider influence most in this diagram?
What should I do differently next time?

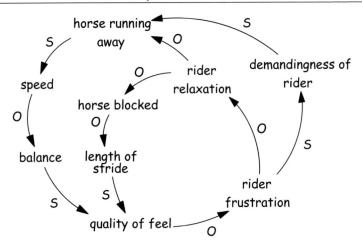

Figure 37 CLD example

Add what you learnt to your "accepted riding wisdom" but be prepared to update and revise it in the light of new information. Accept that what you know now will only ever be "to the best of your current knowledge".

The Learning Zone
Good riding needs physical comfort and mental comfort. Whilst physical comfort is partly about equipment, mental comfort is about understanding. Physical core strength revolves around developing the core muscles deep inside the pelvis at our centre. Mental core strength

is the size of our comfort zone. The core is strong, as it is at the centre of our mind. Outer layers are weaker at the edges and can be very thin, flimsy and fragile! It follows that the place of greatest security is at the very centre.

It follows that the things that are very familiar to us are in our comfort zone. The things that make us anxious are in our fear zone. Somewhere in between there is a zone called the learning zone...where we are operating in unfamiliar territory but with a feeling of safety that keeps us away from the fear zone. No learning happens in our comfort zone. No learning happens in our fear zone (for different reasons). The clever learner operates on the boundaries of the comfort zone – gradually building new areas of comfort in the learning zone but never overstepping the mark into the fear zone. The skilled trainer of humans or horses knows this and works at the boundary in order to put the pupil into a learning situation where they can experience new things safely.

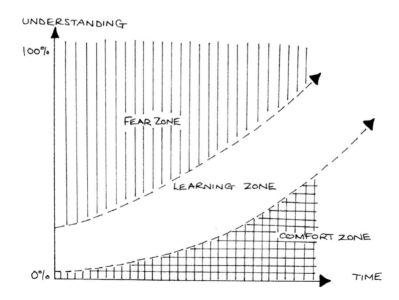

Figure 38 Learning Zones

Comfort, safety, learning and development are very closely connected. To extend our comfort zone we need to understand how to learn. I believe that my comfort comes from depth of understanding. This means that I don't need to have done the thing to feel comfort, but I do need to have understood it and to believe that it can work theoretically.

To understand how a physical thing works eg a car, a house, a boiler, a computer, we can literally dissemble it and understand what affects what. And to do that effectively and efficiently we need the assistance of tools, and sometimes workshop manuals. The skills are manual and involve dexterity.

It's not so easy to do that with a person's head or with a relationship. These are things that are "invisible" and affect our feelings rather than things that we can literally see, touch and feel...but it is essential to understanding. The tools here are cerebral and are about communicating and understanding.

How does safety affect learning?

We can see this in the diagram below. Feeling safe affects our need for stability (o) affects preparedness to experiment (try new things) (o) affects "success"/feeling of achievement (s) affects confidence/"OK-ness" (s) affects feeling safe (s) and we are back where we started!

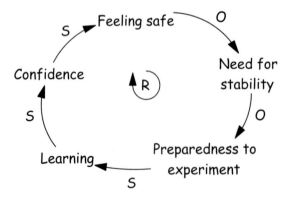

Figure 39 Reinforcing Loop "Security"

Everything begins and ends with safety. This is the core growth and development loop and it is both virtuous and vicious as it is reinforcing. Whatever behaviour we start with will be reinforced – for better or for worse – unless something else changes. Reinforcing loops create exponential behaviour patterns that look like this.

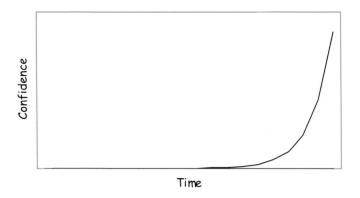

Figure 40 Behaviour of Reinforcing Loops

So we can see that confidence takes a long time to build – for a while it looks like we are achieving nothing and we could give up.

Equally, small losses of confidence (little knocks) can be ignored as insignificant. Remember the frog in the pan of water that is brought slowly to the boil...

Can you think of any similar experiences that have affected you?

Something similar happened to me with my riding. I didn't realise what was happening at the time as it happened over a long time period. First of all, I stopped competing. Then I stopped jumping. Then I stopped hacking out. Slowly but very definitely the world closes in...our comfort zones retreat. We take the knocks and try to patch up the pieces with whatever they have – cover up the damage! Don't bleed – the sharks will smell the blood!

Gradually the knocks build up until eventually we literally "fall off the edge of the cliff" of an exponential decline! The inevitable crash seems out of all proportion to the one small thing before it. Especially if we don't understand the mechanism behind it!

It is fine to support yourself through hard times with "props". But make sure that you have chosen this route consciously and you know that they are not a long term solution. The long term solution is always to think through to the root causes of the problem and fix those slowly and clearly.

Copying
A few maxims, from my experience:
Copying without understanding is dangerous.
Achieving something without understanding is accidental.
Achieving something with understanding is repeatable.
Copying something you've seen someone else do, without understanding of how and why they were doing it, is mindless ignorance.

Who is responsible for the consequences? The copier or the person being copied?

Let's consider an example that is topical in dressage today. Rider A is successful. She rides her horses deep. I also want success. Therefore I must ride my horses deep. In this thinking we have not understood why Rider A is doing this and we don't know how this relates to success. We only think we know what to do (that which we see). It could be that this action is entirely unsuited to our own circumstances (often because we haven't understood them either!)

Adaptation

If we take the time and pay attention we can learn about riding from many other activities and disciplines. Stop regularly and ask yourself, what does xyz teach me about riding?

I enjoy **swimming**. What does swimming teach me about riding?
Here are some of my thoughts:
To become more effective it is necessary to let go in the water and allow the water to support you...it is the same with riding!
If you don't "let go" the water cannot support you and most of your effort with your limbs will be directed to just staying afloat...the same with riding!

To let go when we swim we must trust and embrace the water. To let go when we ride we must trust and embrace the horse.

If we don't trust we cannot let go...

Watch an average adult swimming session. The swimmers are mainly only just capable of staying afloat and yet are expending huge amounts of energy and effort. Their definition of swimming is "staying afloat from A to B". Invariably these swimmers have tight backs and necks. This restricts limb movement and necessitates rapid limb movement to stay afloat. There is a lot of wasted effort.

Often in a group of swimmers you see one swimmer who appears at ease in the water. The movement is graceful, easy and rhythmic. She looks like she can go on forever. It looks like little effort and it is little effort. The other swimmers appear not to notice the experienced swimmer and show no curiosity as to what she is doing differently.

If asked about the lone swimmer the others may remark: the swimmer is a "natural"; the swimmer has a better body structure for swimming; the swimmer has more time to practice than them. They rarely say this swimmer has understood the mechanics of swimming and has given themselves to the water.

More understanding means less effort and so more grace and beauty. Less understanding means more effort, often more force and so more injuries.

What does the lone swimmer feel like in the pool?
- She feels calm, supported and light
- Her brain is primarily feeling not thinking
- She is continually releasing unwanted tension in her muscles
- She maintains a steady rhythm. The rhythm is like a drug; a non-stop dance
- Her breathing is coordinated with the rhythm. It is deep and regular.
- She uses her out breath to let go and wait
- She is aware of her straightness and symmetry left to right and she continually realigns herself
- Nothing in her body blocks the power of her limbs. The energy from behind (the legs) goes right through the body to the tips of the fingers which direct the energy
- She feels good. She feels alive.

What are the adaptations we can take from swimming to riding?

The swimmer has learnt to change "strokes" and not get stuck in any one stroke. The changed stroke gives feedback and stretches different muscle groups. The implication of this is that we should change pace and outline when we work our horses to avoid overworking certain muscle groups.

She has learnt that backstroke requires soft knees. When she stiffens her knees her lower back tightens. She feels this and focuses on releasing the tightness in her knees. Many swimmers curl their neck and head out of the water and allow their bottom to sink. This is inefficient as the curve impedes forward progress. This can be corrected by raising the bottom and relaxing the head and neck back in the water. This really emphasises the need for a mechanically efficient shape to avoid wasted effort. This explains why we need our horse to be "straight".

She has learnt that breast stroke is like "rowing". There is a moment of suspension where we are carried forward by our momentum. Back stroke is like a paddle boat there is no moment of suspension.

She has learnt that swimming in circles is difficult and a figure of eight is very difficult on the change. Swimming in a circle requires the use of mainly the outside arm and inside leg just like riding!

She has learnt that swimming in one place (ie treading water) is easy when relaxed but difficult with effort. A huge effort is always required to move on again if tension has crept in. This must be rather like piaffe for the horse.

She has learnt to warm-up slowly and gradually put in more effort to reach full potential.

She has learnt to cool-down slowly and keep warm after the swim. She eats and drinks afterwards. It is the same for our horse.

She has learnt to experiment and try new techniques. What if I stretch more through my shoulders? What if I really keep my fingers together and arms aligned?

She has learnt from her experiences.

I think that swimming helps us to appreciate what it is like to be a horse being trained for dressage. It also helps us to appreciate the qualities of a good rider/trainer. Swimming builds fitness, suppleness and core strength for riding. It is a symmetrical activity and so helps to build evenness so vital for riding well. Done correctly it helps to loosen the lower back. I would strongly recommend swimming to all riders.

In contrast, my brother rides **motorcycle trials**. The aim is to make it through a section, a marked route which could be outdoors (natural) or indoors (man-made). A stop receives 5 penalties. Using one foot as a support receives 1 penalty. 2 penalties are received for using two feet at the same time or one foot twice. More than two "dabs" but with no loss of forward progression gets a maximum of 3 penalties.

Time and again I am struck by the similarities between riding a horse effectively and riding a trials bike effectively. The top riders have immense core strength. They are incredibly aware of balance – the consequences of a lack of it are so much greater for the trials rider than the dressage rider. The horse can be clever and protect itself and its rider – a bike knows none of these things!

Whilst the trials rider does not sit on a saddle the principles of good posture are evident – shoulder-hip-heel alignment. To rise to the top of the sport the trials rider unites with the bike and develops great "feel". The rider needs to choose a good route through the section. This involves selecting the right gear, the right mix of energy (throttle control), energy control (clutch control) and brakes to ensure the bike stays forwards, straight and in balance! Easy? No. Although a bike is built straight it is still possible to lose straightness in movement when the front wheel becomes misaligned with the path of the rear wheel. As a result the engine loses its ability to drive the bike forwards.

The difference between the bike and the horse is that the new bike comes out of the factory built for trials – the rider can only damage it. No amount of good bike riding will improve the bike. On the contrary the horse is built relatively weakly and with good training we aim to improve his strength and ability to do things.

Well ridden, the trials bike is able to execute the same range of movements as the well ridden horse including jumps (onto and off great heights), airs above the ground, pirouettes on rear and front wheels. It strikes me that the throttle, like the rider's leg, creates energy. The clutch, like the rider's pelvis, controls that energy. The brake (like the rider's hand) is used sparingly and carefully. If it is used too much for the forwards energy you lose the rear wheel. It is interesting that the trials rider learns these things quickly. He has no-one else to blame (stupid horse!) And it hurts a lot more when he gets it wrong!

The trials rider is also acutely aware of the evenness of his weight, side to side. If he leans too much one way the bike is very unforgiving (unlike the stupid horse eh?). I think all riders would benefit from watching or even trying motorbike trials.

What other hobbies/activities do you have?
What do they teach you about riding?

Many riders are obsessive about horses. Horses are their lifestyle. Horses don't leave much time for other interests. I would like to encourage you to take up more activities. Complementary activities such as pilates, swimming, yoga, martial arts will help with your riding.
If you don't have time to fit in other activities observe your partner, friends and family in their activities. Ask yourself, what can I learn that I can apply in my riding? This has two great advantages. First of all riding as a sport is relatively closed minded and this means there is little scope for innovation. Second, if we tie up too much of our self worth in riding what happens when we are unable to do it? Taking part in other activities builds resilience.

Things to remember
Know yourself.
Take responsibility! Don't give power away (eg to trainers, saddlers etc).
Choose consciously. Never react! Stop, breathe deeply, think through the options, make a wiser choice!
Never stop learning. Learn how to be more effective in your learning.
Open and free your mind. Ask more questions.
Seek knowledge. Be discerning: Use Systems Thinking to sort the wheat from the chaff. Choose what makes sense. Store it and use it. Be prepared to challenge it in future.
Learn how to use books.
Understand your learning zone and work to expand it.
Do more activities, especially those complementary to riding, such as swimming and Pilates. Learn from these activities.

Afterword

To all those feeling lost and powerless.
I wrote this book for you.
To help you and your horse find each other and take back your power.

Remember that to control our horse we must first control our self.
Our self is our mind and our body.
We only have one mind and one body. So we must
Nourish, develop and control our minds. And
Nourish, develop and control our bodies.
Take responsibility for yourself and your influence.
The only person you can change is yourself.
Take your power back and make it happen.
Start now... build slowly...and remember you are not alone.
There is always more to learn.............

Appendix 1 - References

(1) FEI, Article 401 Object and General Principles of Dressage, *Rules for Dressage Events*, 22nd edition, effective 1st January 2006, updated 12.01.07, www.horsesport.org

(2) Covey, Stephen R., *The 7 Habits of Highly Effective People,* Running Press (Philadelphia), 1989

(3) Burger, Udo, *The Way to Perfect Horsemanship (tr. Nicole Bartle),* J.A. Allen (London) 1998 (First published as Vollendete Reitkunst, Paul Parey, Berlin and Hamburg 1959)

(4) Herbermann, Erik, *Dressage Formula,* J.A.Allen (London) 1999

(5) Micklem, William, *The Complete Manual of Horse-Riding,* Dorling Kindersley 2003

(6) The German National Equestrian Federation, *The Principles of Riding*, (tr. Christina Belton), Kenilworth Press 1997

(7) Belasik, Paul, *Dressage for the 21st century,* J.A.Allen (London) 2001, (see also www.paulbelasik.com)

(8) Oliveira, Nuno, *Reflections on Equestrian Art* (tr. Phyliss Field), J.A.Allen (London) 1988 (First published as Reflexions sur l'arte Equestre, Crepin Leblond, France, 1964)

(9) Wanless, Mary, *Ride with your Mind Essentials,* Kenilworth Press, 2002 (see also www.mary-wanless.com)

(10) Henriquet, Michel, *Henriquet on Dressage*, Trafalgar Square Publishing, Vermont, 2004, (Tr Hilda Nelson),

(11) Moffett, Heather, *Enlightened Equitation,* David & Charles, 1999, (see also www.enlightenedequitation.com)

(12) Swift , Sally, *Centred Riding,* Trafalgar Square Farm, 1985, *Centred Riding 2,* Trafalgar Square Publishing, 2002 (see also www.centeredriding.org)

(13) Klimke, Ingrid and Reiner, *Basic Training of the Young Horse*, J.A.Allen (London), 1985

(14) Podhajsky, Alois, *The Complete Training of Horse & Rider,* (tr. Eva Podhajsky), The Sportsmans Press (London) 1997 (First published as Die Klassiche Reitkunst, Nymphenburger Verlagshand-lung GmbH., Munich 1965)

(15) Museler, Wilhelm, *Riding Logic* , Eyre Methuen Ltd (London) 1975. (First published as Museler: REITLEHRE, Paul Parey Verlag, Berlin and Hamburg 1937)
(16) Sandin, Theresa, www.sustainabledressage.net
(17) de Kunffy, Charles , *The Athletic Development of the Dressage Horse*, Wiley Publishing (New York), 1992, (see also www.charlesdekunffy.com)
(18) Kyrklund , Kyra, and Lemkow, Jytte, *Dressage with Kyra,* Kenilworth Press Ltd, 1998, (see also www.kyrak.com)
(19) Hempfling , Klaus Ferdinand, *Dancing with Horses,* (tr Kristina McCormack), Trafalgar Square Publishing, 2001, (also see www.hempfling.com)
(20) Harris, Thomas A., *I'm OK - You're OK,* Pan Books Ltd, 1973
(21) Fernyhough, Kate and Watson, Rhona, "*The Dynamic Seat*", British Dressage magazine, Oct/Nov 2005 and Dec/Jan 2006
(22) Harris, Charles, *Fundamentals of Riding*, J.A. Allen (London)
(23) www.bodycontrol.co.uk - the official website of Body Control Pilates
(24) Kelly , Emily, *Commonsense Pilates,* Anness Publishing Ltd, 2001
(25) MacDonnell, Michèle, *Alexander Technique* , Anness Publishing Ltd 1999
(26) Senge, Peter M., *The Fifth Discipline*, Doubleday (New York), 1990
(27) Sherwood, Dennis, *Seeing the Forest for the Trees* , Nicholas Brealey Publishing, 2002
(28) www.globaldressageforum.com – see under section on "dressage terms" for glossary of terms for dressage.
(29) Niggli, Wolfgang M, *Dressage a guideline for judges and riders*, J.A.Allen (London) 2003
(30) www.stat.org.uk - the official website of the Society for Teachers of the Alexander Technique. The definitive guide to the Alexander Technique.
(31) Baucher, Francois, *New Method of Horsemanship*, in Nelson, H., *Francois Baucher the man and his method*, J.A.Allen (London) 1992
(32) Weis, Richard, and Miesner, Susanne, *The Posture does the Riding*, on www.richardweis.com.
(33) Quote from survey response of Mal Phillips. Mal Phillips began riding at the age of 2, and has been a fascinated observer of equine

behaviour ever since. He is a listed panel judge for both Dressage and
Veteran Horse Society shows.
(34) Quote from survey response of Andrea Hessay. Andrea is an
experienced competition rider (dressage & eventing) and BHSI-SM,
BHSII.
(35) Quote from survey response of Hilda Rodger.
Hilda is an equestrian consultant. She can be contacted via her website
at www.thenaturalapproach.co.uk, where she also sells books, numnahs,
herbs, homeopathic remedies and other quality products for people, pets
and horses.
(36) www.vensim.com - the website of Ventana Systems inc. Download of
Vensim systems dynamics software (including a personal learning version
for free)
(37) www.barefoothorse.com - advice on caring for your horse's feet.
(38) www.eatwell.gov.uk - government recommended nutrition guidelines.
www.food.gov.uk - the Food Standards Agency "Safe food and healthy
eating for all"
(39) www.pegasuscom.com - systems thinking resources
(40) www.bhs.org.uk - the official website of the British Horse Society
(41) www.britishdressage.co.uk - the official website of British Dressage
(42) www.dodsonandhorrell.com/uk/dh/horse - Dodson & Horrell
Limited. Feed, supplements and herbal products for horses and award
winning advice and information.

Other recommended web sites
www.kerryturner.net - the author's website.
www.abrs.org.uk - the official website of the Association of British
Riding Schools.
www.idrc.de - the official website of the International Dressage Riders
Club.
www.allege-ideal.com - International Dressage & Equitation Association
for Lightness.

Appendix 2 - Survey questions

The following questions were sent tot a large group of trainers, riders and judges. Their responses are used throughout the book.

1. What are you aiming to achieve when training horses and training riders?

2. How does this differ in the short vs the long term?

3. How do you know when you've achieved these goals? What are the things that help you to achieve these goals? What gets in the way?

4. How would your approach differ for horses/riders with physical or mental problems?

5. Which riders and trainers do you most admire and why?

6. Which riders and trainers do you least admire and why?

7. Who has most influenced your philosophy on training horses and riders? How?

8. Are there any books/videos/websites you would recommend to those interested in training horses and riders?

9. What words of advice would you give to an owner-rider with a full-time non-equestrian job aiming to improve her riding and her horse?

10. How do you feel (in your mind and your body) when you are riding at your best?

11. What are the most important attributes of a good rider?

12. You are a dressage judge! How would you judge a rider who rode her horse and did all the test movements perfectly - her horse

is truly engaged behind and in a beautiful outline in front (light and easy on the forehand; loose through the shoulders; soft in the neck) where the reins are like a thread of silk (picture I am thinking of is Nuno Oliveira - the reins *just* slack. See photos in "Reflections on Equestrian Art".) - BUT a slight loop always in the reins. What collective marks and comments would you give?

13. How do you feel that competitive dressage (British Dressage) has influenced the quality of training horses and riders?

14. How do you feel that the British Horse Society has influenced the quality of training horses and riders in Great Britain?

15. What, if anything, would you change to improve the system of training horses and riders in Great Britain?

16. Why do you... Train horses? Train riders? Compete? Judge?

17. What other questions would you want to add to this list?

18. Are there any other trainers you think should contribute to this survey (do you have contact details)?

Appendix 3 - Pilates

An interview with Kate Fernyhough and Rhona Watson.

Q: *What is Pilates?*
A: Pilates is an holistic exercise regime, focusing on the awareness and strengthening of the inner core / stability muscles of the trunk and joints. The exercises incorporate a series of strengthening, stretching, balance and awareness principles and facilitate coordination, relaxation and enhanced body control.

Q: *What are the aims of Pilates?*
A: The aims of Pilates are many, but primarily involve the re-education and relearning of normal movement patterns that enable the body to function most efficiently. This includes enhancing patterns of breathing, muscle recruitment and coordination skills.

Q: *How does Pilates help the rider?*
A: The re-education of movement patterns and fine tuning of body senses teaches the rider to become more aware of the subtle changes in their position and balance on the horse. Pilates teaches ideal body alignment and symmetry, and enables the rider to develop the suppleness and specific strength in the spine and pelvis to absorb the equine pelvic movements and work with the equine movement, rather than against it. Developing a "dynamic riding seat" enables enhanced upper body function, and most importantly, active release of unnecessary tension and tightness in inappropriate muscle groups. A true, independent seat is established.

Q: *How does the rider use pilates when riding, lunging and working in the stables?*
A: Pilates is a whole programme of activities that needs to be learnt from the basics. The essence of Pilates is that the bad habits or faulty movement patterns must first be unlearnt, and then the correct movements and muscle sequences learnt and repeated over and over until they become natural. The basic principles such as corrected standing

and sitting postures, and breathing techniques, can and must be practised at any time if the bad habits are to be changed. Changing repetitive asymmetrical activities such as shovelling and carrying heavy buckets should be practised equally with both sides or with both arms. Pilates principles are best practised little and often in a variety of positions whilst riding. Most importantly it should be practiced during activities of daily life.

Q: *How does Pilates fit with other exercise regimes?*
A: Pilates should form the basis of all forms of exercise from cardiovascular training in a gym to playing sports. Many fitness regimes are unspecific and serve only to reinforce the bad habits and faulty movement patterns already present. When Pilates principles are applied, the maximum benefit can be gained from the activity whatever that might be.

Q: *How does Pilates fit with other therapy regimes eg physiotherapy, osteopathy?*
A: The principles of Pilates training are very popular with most therapy regimes as they reinforce and extend the benefits of the therapy. Many therapists refer clients to Pilates during, or most commonly after, the course of treatment. Retraining the core muscle strength and mobilising restricted movements is an essential part of the recovery, and there may not be an opportunity within the treatment sessions to focus on these elements sufficiently.

Q: *How does Pilates fit with other mind/body regimes eg Alexander Technique?*
A: There are many similarities and much overlap with Pilates and other mind body regimes, which serves to reinforce the importance of this combined approach to training. Each regime has a specific target area, but the unique benefit is the enhanced body awareness gained by using a mind and body approach.

Q: *What is the best way to learn Pilates?*
A: Ideally as with any specific exercise regime, Pilates is best learned on a one to one basis. Even if this is not possible an initial assessment

with a recognised Pilates trainer is essential. No two clients will require the same specific instructions, although in a group class situation it is possible to cover the most common movement faults and scenarios.

Q: *Is it better to learn Pilates individually or in a group?*
A: There is a lot to be gained from weekly attendance at a group Pilates session, although working on an individual level with a client obviously enables a more specific approach. If group attendance is the only option, then it is very important to select a Pilates teacher who limits the class numbers to no more than 12, to ensure that you get some individual attention within the class. There are several schools of Pilates in the UK who insist on small group numbers, the most well known and recognised being the "Body Control Pilates Association"

Q: *Is it better for riders to learn Pilates from an instructor who is riding aware?*
A: Obviously the more specific the knowledge regarding the sport, the more benefit to the individual, however there are too few Pilates instructors with rider knowledge at present, and some Pilates exercise is far better than none. The benefits gained through Pilates require much learning and practice, and it is suggested that it takes at least 3 months before any real benefit is experienced. The initial principles of Pilates can be taught to a beginner by a non riding Pilates instructor, and a more specific approach taken once the early knowledge has been practiced and consolidated.

Q: *How do you know you are doing it right?*
A: As with riding instruction, you may not know initially whether you are doing the Pilates exercises correctly, but with progressive learning, close supervision and practise, recognition of the correct movement patterns will feel familiar. These familiar movements and actions can then be built upon, and the individual gains better body awareness leading to greater knowledge. It is only with repetition under supervision and this enhanced body awareness, that the correct patterns will be learned well enough to be practised without supervision.

Q: *Are there any particular exercises you would recommend for riders? Mounted and dismounted?*

A: There are many exercises specific for the rider, but it is essential to firstly learn the basic principles of Pilates, and that information cannot be taught from a book alone. Trying to copy exercises from script or a static picture may only lead to reinforcement of the faulty patterns already present, and little will be gained. There are many well presented books and DVDs highlighting the basic principles and basic exercises, but it is still advisable to seek the individual attention of a well qualified teacher.

Q: *Is it possible for me to teach my horse Pilates? How?*

A: If you are learning and practising good groundwork and dressage training, you are already teaching your horse many of the principles of training that Pilates offer the rider. It is almost possible to consider Pilates as dressage training for the rider. One of the most obvious benefits of dressage training for the horse is the enhanced awareness and sensitivity to the aids that you instil. Only with this increase in proprioception will you and the horse be able to progress on to more challenging moves and better dressage scores.

Q: *Is there an ideal body shape for a rider? What is it?*

A: There is no absolute ideal body shape for riders, but some body features can pose a challenge! Features such as short stocky legs, or a top heavy upper body can be a mechanical disadvantage, but on the other hand a well constructed rider may lack the rider performance and therefore restrict the abilities of the horse. Our body shape is on the whole difficult to change radically, although weight loss has a huge implication for balance and mobility. Of greater importance possibly, is the combined choice of the rider and horse team. It would seem more appropriate for example, to select a mount with a suitable riding action for a very short stout rider.

Q: *Do dressage riders need cardiovascular fitness? What do you recommend to build the necessary cv fitness?*

A: General fitness is an essential requirement for activities of daily life, let alone for performance in sport. Cardio vascular fitness is important in maintaining suppleness, strength and general health and should be considered an essential part of rider training. This does not mean that every rider should employ a personal trainer and attend the gym 3 times a week. Simple cardio vascular activities include walking further and quicker over regular routes, climbing stairs, running on the spot for 1 minute bursts, and are easy and convenient to perform regularly at no added expense. It is advisable that we each should attempt to get slightly out of breath at least once a day. Riders do need to consider the sports and activities that they practise. Try to select symmetrical activities such as swimming rather than tennis and squash which reinforce asymmetrical muscle function.

Q: *Many riders I know have lower back problems (typically discs). Does riding cause this? What do you recommend for riders with back problems?*
A: I personally do not feel that riding is responsible for many riders having bad backs. Indeed, if the rider is correctly balanced, and has developed a true, independent seat, then riding can act positively upon the spinal joints. Most adults will experience an episode of back pain at some point in their life, and back pain is the most common reason for a GP visit. It may be the activities of stable management and the additional strain on the lower back that is more responsible for the high incidence of back pain. Disc related back pain is also more common in the younger and middle aged adult. Back pain must be treated and managed well to avoid the onset of a chronic problem. Individuals must also be more responsible for managing their own symptoms long term, and not rely so much on the medical approach for a quick fix for their problems. The Pilates principles of strengthening the core musculature and re-educating movement patterns play a huge part in maintaining a healthier spine.

Q: *Have you read Betsy Steiner's book "Gymnastic dressage Training using the mind, body and spirit"? If so, what do you agree with and what do you see differently? Why?*
A: Yes I have read Betsy Steiner's book, and in fact went out to Florida several years ago to spend a week with Betsy and undertake her first

"Equilates" training course. I was most impressed by her approach and can only support the detail and content of her book. My only reservation from a Pilates aspect is the availability in the UK of the machine based Pilates exercises highlighted in the book. If more riders want to use Pilates, it would more appropriate to use more mat based versions of the exercises, to make the approach more user friendly.

Q: *Anything else to add?*
A: I would like to add that the concept of developing a rider based regime of assessment and exercise using the well practised principles of Pilates is foremost in the work that myself and my colleagues from "The Dynamic Riding" team are presently working on in the UK. We are presently developing a programme of clinics and workshops for 2006/2007, along with appropriate support material, DVD's etc..............

For further information please contact Kate Fernyhough at eccleshall.physio@fsmail.net.

Appendix 4 - Osteopathy

An interview with Dustie Houchin.

Dustie Houchin qualified from the British School of Osteopathy in 1998; graduating as an Animal Osteopath in 2001. She is the founder of three Osteopathic practices in the South East of England , including one in Harley Street . She also works in conjunction with three Veterinary Practices covering a broad geographical area with her equine and canine work. Her animal patients range from pets to professional Show Horses and she also works voluntarily to help animals in need.

In 2006 Dustie studied an Advanced Management Programme at Ashridge, followed by an MBA at Warwick Business School & SDA Bocconi. Today she mixes Clinical practice with Business Consulting, helping existing practitioners and graduates to build strong successful practices and networks by designing personalized businesses packages which allow them to do what they love most; treating patients.

Q: *What is osteopathy?*

A: Osteopathy is a complete and well established healthcare system, which teaches the following philosophy. The body is a unit in and of itself, which has its own self regulating and protecting mechanisms and its structure and function are mutually interrelated. The system of Osteopathic examination and treatment is therefore built upon these principles and one of the main aims is to allow the body to heal itself.

Osteopaths use many of the standard clinical and orthopaedic assessments which allow clarity of diagnosis. They are interested in each individual as an individual and every case history is viewed as unique. They assess the mechanical, functional and posture aspects of the patient's body and intertwine that information with what is known of the patient's social and working environment, thus assessing the whole picture and not just a snapshot in time.

Q: *Who can benefit from it?*

A: Anyone can benefit from Osteopathy. It is a system which can be used either for people with specific problems or for those who wish to maintain a balanced and healthy body. Many of us walk around with minor aches and pains, and do not exercise or stretch as much as we should. We push ourselves both physically and mentally and do not rest adequately. All this leads to an imbalance in our structure and the function our body, which generally results in pain and stiffness. So whether you are an athlete or a house-wife; twenty years old or sixty, Osteopathy can help you keep your body performing to the best of its ability.

Q: *What problems do riders (horses) come to you with?*

A: I treat a wide variety of muscular-skeletal problems, ranging from injuries caused by day to day activities associated with owning a horse, and others which stem from a simple lack of fitness and readiness for the sport. People wouldn't try to run a marathon without training and they shouldn't take up riding and/or a new discipline expecting their body to adapt instantly. I see so many riders who become stiff and sore and yet continue to ride without adequate physical training. Eventually these imbalances are transferred to the horse during riding, and the horse has to compensate for the rider's discrepancy. This can cause problems with the horse's own biomechanics and a cycle begins.

Many of the problems I see are caused because the rider is unfit for the sport, lacking general muscular tone and internal muscular strength. Many riders mount their horse and switch off physically, expecting the horse to provide all the energy and enthusiasm. When I say this I am of course referring to the amateur rider, not the professional (although I have seen my fair share of unfit professionals too).

Riders need to be pro-active when they ride, using their posture correctly and maintaining a soft neutral spinal position, with abdominal tone engaged at all times. Legs should have a firm, gentle enveloping contact and arms and shoulders should be relaxed, as tension in this area leads to all sorts of problems in the upper back and neck region. Riders should also be balanced in their seat bones when riding, as imbalances in the seat can have a huge impact on the horse's own balance.

As I see it, all riders need a good teacher to assess their position and alignment when riding, and someone to encourage the correct use of the body. Riding requires a degree of physical tone and one should be both generally fit and riding fit. Working on the strength of the legs, back and abdominals can really help to improve overall control and also the intensity of movement required thus making the overall experience of riding much more enjoyable; both for the rider and the horse.

Q: *Have you noticed any patterns?*

A: Only really those I mention above which relate to poor physical condition.

Otherwise I study each individual as they present in my surgery, with their own set of social, physical and mental issues. Some may present with a direct injury from a fall or a blow, whereas others may be suffering merely from the aches and pains associated with the hard labour of horse ownership.

Of course the back and neck are always going to be target areas for riders because of the nature of the sport, but because levels of fitness and skill can be so varied, it is almost impossible to group people together. For example, professionals suffer very differently from say a total beginner and those who study dressage will have different probable injuries to those who ride cross country courses.

Q: *What do you believe causes these problems?*

A: A lack of readiness for the sport and/or chosen discipline, with those who simply own a horse for the purpose of hacking out being at most risk, because they generally don't have lessons, so bad habits escalate very quickly.

As far as I can see, many of the problems that arise for riders are as a result of limited technical information and training along with a body that is less than appropriately ready for the tasks demanded of it.

Q: *What body factors do you believe influence a rider's capability to ride well?*

A: I think there is little doubt that those who perform well have a greater degree of general fitness and muscular tone than those who take their riding a little less seriously. Good abdominal tone and a strong back help tremendously with riding technique and balance, and strong leg muscles aid in the control and precision of movements, and help to avoid excessive use of the upper back.

Riding is a very physical sport when performed well. It uses every aspect of the body, from the pelvic floor to the base of the neck. A good rider uses muscular tone rather than brute force to attain the required movement in the horse. Movements should be subtle and gentle both for the rider and the horse. This way the horse does not become confused by the bombardment of signals and is able to listen to the riders aids easily and effectively.

Riding from a physical point of view is about balance, tone, fitness and breath. All of which are required to achieve the maximum physical relationship between horse and rider. If a rider bounces around, unable to control their own centre of balance, unable to maintain a good seat, incapable of using abdominal tone to drive their horse forward and breathing frantically due to a lack of fitness, what hope has the poor horse got of doing anything well.

A horse ideally needs to be supported by a rider with a firm but gentle leg, a good seat, balanced posture, calm breathing and an energised level of tone that tells the horse that he can perform to the best of his ability without losing his rider. I often think of riding as I do Osteopathy, it is about balance of structure and function and about acting as a single unit not as disengaged parts of a whole.

Q: *What exercises/therapies would you recommend for riders? Is there anything you would specifically recommend immediately before or after a riding session?*

A: Core stability exercises on a fit ball are excellent for correcting a rider's seat and improving the internal abdominal and spinal stabilizers. These exercises can be taught by a therapist or at a gym under the guidance of an instructor. They are very subtle exercises but have tremendous end results.

Also, as I have mentioned, a general fitness regime of cardio-vascular training and strength training is helpful for any level of rider because it makes the whole process of riding more enjoyable.

Stretching is also an important component of any exercise regime and whilst stretching is often confused with fitness, it is a completely separate entity. Good flexibility allows the body to move more fluidly and with less risk of injury. Basic yoga is also an option for those who have the time to attend a class, but it is really important to find a class to suit the individual's needs. Yoga encompasses exercises of balance, breathing, strength and flexibility, all of which would benefit a rider.

Pre-riding – I would always suggest that a rider stretches before riding. Simply working through the back, quadriceps, hamstrings and calf muscles and once mounted, stretching the inside leg away, in order to lengthen the leg before placing it in the stirrup. This frees up the body and creates a sense of length.

Of course, in an ideal world, proper warm ups and spinal exercises would be of benefit; but as most riders are pushed for time and do not have any private space at the yards for such activity, it is mostly unsuitable to even suggest it.

Q: *There is a lot of heavy work involved in caring for horses. Are there any guidelines you would give for this?*

A: The stronger the person is, the less likely they are to become injured. So follow all the rules above.

Always lift correctly using the strength of the legs and bending one's knees whilst maintaining a straight back is the safest position for moving heavy objects.

Q: *Can regular osteopathy help a rider? How? How often?*

A: Osteopathy can help maintain the fluidity of movement within a rider's body, helping to avoid restrictions that might otherwise become problematic.

Q: *How does osteopathy fit with - Pilates; Alexander technique; Physiotherapy; sports massage; Yoga; Tai Chi; Gym; aerobics/step; jogging; swimming; racket sports.*

A: I have been in practice for some 15 years as a Sports Therapist and Osteopath, and I treat both humans and horses. Over the years I have come to realise that each patient has their own set of needs. Some need to focus on flexibility and thus Yoga is ideal, others need a fitness overhaul and would gain from going to the gym two or three times a week. From a treatment perspective, again it is somewhat individual and also about cost. In an ideal world I would work with an Alexander technique teacher and a sports masseuse/masseur, but many people struggle to afford one treatment, let alone three; so I tend to refer patients on, as and when appropriate, and this seems to work quite well.

Q: *Are there any supports (back; sacroiliac etc) you would recommend for riders?*

A: Not ideally. The answer is....get fitter.

Q: *Are there any machines e.g. massage, TENs or lotions/potions you would recommend for riders?*

A: There are a multitude of lotions and potions on the market but ultimately it is the massage that is required to apply them that does the most good, so if you have sore muscles have a good soak in a warm bath and ask someone to give you a gentle massage. If something is swollen or painful however, a therapist or doctor should be visited in order for a proper diagnosis to be made.

Ice is a helpful tool for acute injury but the pack should always be covered with a tea-towel or something similar and applied for a maximum of ten minutes (five on less fleshy areas).

Machines such as TENS are available but should be used under the guidance of a therapist.

Appendix 5 - Massage

An interview with Phil Ward. Phil is a sports and remedial masseur based in Giggleswick, North Yorkshire. He treats a wide range of patients, who come to him with a variety of injuries and ailments. He is also a qualified Mountain Leader and rock climbing enthusiast, and regularly competes in mountain marathons and other endurance events.

Q: *What problems do riders come to you with? Have you noticed any patterns? What do you believe causes these problems?*

A: Most of the treatments I have given to riders have been as a result of falls, among them fractured vertebra and collar bones, deep bruising and a whole range of injuries, particularly upper body, from impact.

I have treated some riders for postural problems concerned with balance, not just balance as in the ability to balance, but imbalances in the body, side to side and front to back. Some of these have been a by-product of mounting only from the left, which has caused what is in essence a repetitive strain injury in the lower thoracic area.

Q: *What body factors influence a rider's capability to ride well?*

A: Good balanced muscle power is essential, especially in the pelvic area, the adductors, and the hip flexors and extensors. These are the groups most concerned with control of the riding posture as far as I have observed but you probably can recognise this better than me.

Q: *Are there any supports (back; sacroiliac etc) you would recommend for riders?*

A: I know of no specific supports for riders but that doesn't mean that there are none!

Q: *Are there any machines eg massage, TENs or lotions/potions you would recommend for riders?*

A: A good old fashioned faradic machine will help with muscle power and tone but the best exercise is actually riding. Building up the strengths slowly, allowing time for recovery is a sound principle for any sport and also applies to recovery from injury.

Q: *There is a lot of heavy work involved in caring for horses. Are there any guidelines you would give for this?*

A: The heavy work involved in horses involves the same message. However I would encourage anyone without ingrained habits to learn to shovel and sweep both left and right handed. This will build up equal strengths and hopefully prevent imbalances and overuse problems.

Q: *How does massage fit with - Pilates; Alexander technique; Physiotherapy; Yoga; Tai Chi; Gym; aerobics/step; jogging; swimming; racket sports.*

A: All the disciplines you mentioned are valuable to general welfare as well as riding fitness. You don't need me to tell you the benefits. My speciality, massage contributes in an all round way both for recovery from injury and for event preparation. Warming up and down are as important for the rider as the horse and physical treatment of the appropriate kind (ice, massage support etc) before and after performance should, but rarely are, be regarded as part of the whole experience.

Biographies

Kerry Turner started riding at the age of 11. She gave up ponies in pursuit of academic excellence, achieving a first class honours degree in Mathematics, a Masters degree in Operational Research (applying analytical techniques in business decision making) and a host of prizes and awards. She joined business advisory services firm, Deloitte Haskins & Sells, in 1985. Over the next 20 years, she grew a successful performance management service-line within the consultancy. Analytical techniques, in particular, Systems Thinking, and a quest for the truth, underpinned her work in many global organisations.

She took up riding again in 1992. She competed her own Part-bred Arab, Shantie, in all 3 disciplines. She was an active member of Hitchin Riding Club representing the club in national team competitions and organising dressage competitions for club members. She was also a founder member and chairperson of Ampthill & District Bridleways Association. Achievements here included successfully fighting a local bridleway closure and raising money through sponsored rides to support bridleway maintenance. Her drive to improve her knowledge of horses lead her to Moulton College to study to British Horse Society stage 4 part-time.

She suffered from lower back problems. In her search for help she studied the Alexander Technique as a pupil of Gloria Pullan (senior tutor at STAT). More recently she has been learning Bodycontrol Pilates with a trainer in France. Her growing interest in dressage led her to seek guidance from John Micklem (Irish event trainer), Inger Bryant (Swedish List 1 Judge) and to study as a trainee judge with British Dressage. Kerry's passion for learning saw her travelling the country to attend lectures, demos and training events on her favourite subject. Her passion for learning is well matched by her passion for sharing. Kerry has written a number of articles over the years, many of which have been published in "Horse & Rider" magazine.

In 2005 Kerry decided to leave the business world and to start a new career in writing. In this, her first book, Kerry applies the techniques she used to understand and improve business performance to do the same for riding.

Kerry can be contacted via her website at www.kerryturner.net.

Anne Fenn has been obsessed with ponies since the age of ten. Her passion was fuelled by half hour Saturday riding lessons, which rapidly expanded to spending whole weekends helping out at the riding school. These days provided endless material on which to base written school homework (illustrations, of course, being essential).

On leaving school Anne was adamant that she was going to work with horses. She trained for her BHSAI as a working pupil with Mrs J Leggett at Arundel Riding School. She completed her training and exams at Wellington Riding. Following this she practised for several years as a riding instructor and stable manager.

More recently, Anne gained an HNC in Equine Studies by distance learning with Warwickshire College. She became a registered identifier for the Horse Passport Agency and a nutritional advisor for a leading UK horse feed manufacturer.

Drawing horses has consistently been Anne's 'after dark' pastime and she is now developing this talent as an occupation.

Anne can be contacted by email at anne.fenn.fenn@btinternet.com.

Index

acceptance, 20, 73
adaptation, 221-225
Alexander Technique, 134-136
attention, 95-96
balance, 89-95
Baucher, Francois, 116, 229
behind the vertical, 66-67
Belasik, Paul, 48, 76, 84, 118, 148, 158, 161, 166, 228
breathe, breathing, 84-85, 110, 134
Bryant, Inger, 18, 98, 107, 120, 128,
Burger, Udo, 24, 205, 228
calmness, 48-55, 109-110, 122
canter, 97, 156-158
causal loop diagram, (CLD), 40-41
collection, 114-118
communication, 26, 96-102
competition, 162-163
concentration, 56
connection, 47->, 52-57
contact, 58->
copying, 220
Covey, Stephen, 22, 90, 228
decontraction, 109, 121-122
de Kunffy, Charles, 145, 229
definiteness, 104
dressage, 18
driver tree, 40
engagement, 148, 160
equilibrium, 42
feedback, 36-39
FEI, 18, 58, 228
Fernyhough, Kate, 229, 233-238
fitness, 138-139
focus, 85-86
give & retake, 86-88
giravolta, 148, 156
girth, 194, 197

Global Dressage Forum, 114, 123, 229
half halt, 73, 159
halt, 73, 100-101, 152
harmony, 7, 52
Harris, Charles, 193, 229
Harris, Thomas, 127, 229
Hempfling, Klaus Ferdinand, 64, 166, 188, 193, 229
Henriquet, Michel, 75, 95, 158, 214, 228
Herbermann, Erik, 113, 228
impulsion, 112, 120, 149
Klimke, Reiner, 18, 200, 228
knowledge, 213-216
Kyrklund, Kyra, 159, 229
learning cycle, 208-210
learning rider, 207-208
leg position, 83-84
leg yield, 155
leverage, 45
lunging, 141-144, 200-201, 203-204
massage, 152, 246-247
mental model, 31-32
Micklem, John, 17, 111, 122, 176, 252
Micklem, William, 64, 83, 98, 189, 200
Moffett, Heather, 75, 187, 205, 228
motorcycle trials, 223
Museler, Wilhelm, 129, 229
Niggli, Wolfgang, 114, 229
noseband, 189-191
numnah, 194-196
Oliveira, Nuno, 59, 64, 228, 232
osteopathy, 239-245
outline, 9, 129, 147, 160
persistence, 104
Pilates, 132-134, 233-238

Podhajsky, Alois, 102, 114, 191, 228
reading, 214-215
rein back, 155
rein equilibrium, 68-69
relationship (between variables),
33-34
relaxation, 32, 109
Sandin, Theresa, 115, 149, 204, 229
safety, 217-220
scales of training, 112-114
seat, 77-85
self carriage, 87, 95
Senge, Peter, 46, 229
straightness, 118-119
submission, *see acceptance*
suppleness, 74, 113

Swift, Sally, 86, 91, 214, 228
swimming, 10, 221-223
system, 23-25
Systems Thinking, 32-41, 215-216
tension, 52, 109
thinking funnel, 211-212
tracking up, 161
transitions, 42, 97, 149, 154, 160
trot, 158-161
variable, 32-33
Vensim, 120, 230
walk, 146, 152
Wanless, Mary, 64, 65, 83, 228
Weis, Richard, 125, 136, 229
wisdom, 210